GENDER STUDIES IN INFORMATICS
AN APPLICATION OF SCIENTOMETRIC INDICATORS AND MAPPING TECHNIQUES

GENDER STUDIES IN INFORMATICS

AN APPLICATION OF SCIENTOMETRIC INDICATORS AND MAPPING TECHNIQUES

M.Suriya
Professor &University Librarian, Dept of LIS, Annamalai University
C.Sambandam
Deputy Librarian, University library, Annamalai University
L.N.Umadevi
Asst.Professor, Dept of LIS, Annamalai University
V.Ganesh
Programmer, University Library, Annamalai University
R.Vijay Arumugam
Programmer, University Library, Annamalai University

Ess Ess Publications
New Delhi

Gender Studies in Informatics: An Application of Scientometric Indicators and Mapping Techniques

ISBN: 978-81-7000-649-7

Rs.400/-

First Published 2011

Published by:
Ess Ess Publications
4837/24, Ansari Road,
Darya Ganj,
New Delhi-110 002.
INDIA
Phones: 23260807, 41563444
Fax: 41563334
E-mail: info@essessreference.com
www.essessreference.com

Cover Design by *Patch Creative Unit*

Printed and bound in India at Salasar Imaging Systems.

Contents

1 Introduction 1

2 Review of Literature 9

3 Research Design 20

4 Results and Discussions 29

5 Findings and Conclusion 117

Bibliography 129

Preface

The information economy has flourished and is now evolving into a networking economy that is radically transforming the world of work. But will this revolution be a powerful vehicle for gender equality, or will increasing numbers of women find themselves caught on the wrong side of the digital divide?

The ILO's World Employment Report 2001 "Life at work in the Information Economy", suggests that the development of information and communication technologies (ICTs) offers many new opportunities for women. But unless these are supported by deliberate policies to ensure participation, ownership, education and ICT training for women - as well as family-friendly policies in the information economy workplace - the old gender biases will persist.

Information and communication technologies have created new types of work that favour women because the technology enables work to be brought to homes and allowes for better accommodation of work and family schedules. Women have also been able to capture a large proportion of jobs in ICT enabled services because of the worldwide shortage of skills necessary for work in this sector.

The ILO reports that "telecentres and fax booths have created a quarter of a million jobs in India in the last four years alone, a huge proportion of which have gone to women".

The ILO Report adds that "in terms of numbers employed, the role of women in the digital economy has become more marked in on-line, export-oriented information-processing work rather than in telecommuting.

The Grameen Bank Village Phone Project, which provides cell phones to its mostly female members in Bangladesh, demonstrates not only the employment-generating impact of the women who collect fees for the usage of their mobile phones, but other positive spill-over effects as well. Mobile phones and access to the Internet have given rural Bangladeshi women access to learning, created new opportunities for autonomy and improved their position in community and public life.

Despite the enabling potential ICTs have to improve women's lives, the ILO Report describes a digital divide within countries which broadly reflects the gender divide.

Women's substantial under-representation in the core ICT science and engineering curricula in education systems, means that they are excluded for core ICT occupations. But the Report finds that the gender divide is not consistent across Europe. "While the UK, for example, has one of the lowest proportions of female university students in maths and computer science courses, female enrollment in Italy and Spain at university-level in these subjects is far greater, and women comprise around 50 per cent of their ICT workforces.

In the UK and US, the proportion of women in IT courses is less than 20 per cent of all studying computer science courses at both undergraduate and post-graduate levels, and the percentage seems to be declining further still. Enrollment in Micosoft-certified courses appears to confirm the industry stereotype in that it is dominated by young men, with only 11 per cent of the students being women".

The report finds that educational differences underlie

the different rates of ICT diffusion and Internet usage, leading to the conclusion that "the promotion of education and literacy generally - and digital literacy in particular - is the huge challenge facing all countries. Equipping workers with ICT-related skills will need to be specifically targeted to the needs of women".

The ILO Report finds that patterns of gender segregation are being reproduced in the information economy where men hold the majority of high-skilled, high value-added jobs, whereas women are concentrated in the low-skilled, lower value-added jobs. In addition, the report notes that "the diffusion of the technologies has been skill-biased and thus accompanied by rising wage inequalities. Although pay inequality exists between those who have ICT skills and those who do not, pay polarization also exists within ICT use itself. This polarization is often gender-based".

This book is an attempt to map the status of women in the ICT industries across the globe and also the barriers they have encountered within the industries.

- Authors

1
Introduction

This study focus on mapping the research dynamics of the field gender issues in informatics. It aims at evaluating the research activity of the countries on gender development in informatics by means of their bibliographic output. In recent years there have been a rapid growing interest in the use of quantitative parameters for assessing the quality of research carried out in research institutions, Universities and so on. The need for the study is realized to identify the existing research trends, thrust areas, priorities, gaps and future requirements.[1]

Last two decades have witnessed an overwhelming volume of publications pertaining to gender issues in informatics. Hence, the system of storage and retrieval of information in the process of scientific communication has now become more complex than ever. Not only the exponential growth of literature, but also the inter-disciplinary nature and specialization of research have posed many problems both to the information seekers and librarians. Further emphasis on national and international information systems have signified the need for an analysis of literature used by the scientists.[2]

This study is designed to analyze the research out put

pertaining to the gender issues in the field of informatics and to map the factors attributing to the alarming gender gap and a paucity of women's participation in this field.

Gender in informatics related to information technology and its impact on women's education, training and employment. This study makes special attention on the performance of research output in Gender Studies in Informatics. Today information technology is gaining momentum throughout the globe and extent to which this industry provides employment and livelihood for women in different parts of the world. These issues could be learnt from the publication output.[3]

The analysis is based on the emergence of research areas, research groups and countries with a view to map the cognitive or intellectual structure of research. Further this study spells out the relationship between authors, institutions, journal articles and as a means of assisting the peer review procedure.[4]

The research is based on the published literature on the subject gender issues in informatics. The mapping process consists of conversion of these publication records into a bibliographic database in English language. The co-word mapping technique is used to capture the dimension of knowledge structure or cognitive themes in the field of informatics. This technique consist of building keyword index from the bibliographic database, computing co-occurrence of keywords and measuring the similarity of keywords, cutting up the keyword associations network into clusters, classifying the documents into clusters and building scatter diagrams or maps.

The analysis of growth of literature in gender issues in informatics is an important aspect of this study. It could be observed that the growth of literature has made it difficult for (i) the Scientists to keep in touch with the latest advances in their discipline;(ii) the library professionals to meet the information needs of scientists in various disciplines due to increase in cost of publications and shrinking library budget, and (iii) the policy makers to decide on priorities in resource allocation for scientific activities. If published literature is taken as measure of knowledge, the bibliometric study of these publications would yield useful results regarding the growth pattern of literature in gender issues in informatics. These results are of practical value to the scientists, library professionals and planners in the management of scientific activities in the discipline.[5]

The study of author productivity is an important aspect. The performance of scientists could be viewed in terms of their productivity. Productivity is referred to as the amount of research output and publication that a researcher has done. It is often measured by counting the number of papers, books, reviews and reports produced by a scientist over a period of time. Productivity of a scientist has been linked to various factors such as subject specialization, economic indicators, institutional prestige, promotion and monetary rewards. In general the above factors play a significant role in output performance among the scientists of Western nations. As a result the majority of the world research papers have been published in a few advanced countries of the world. Contrastingly little attention has been paid to the scientific output and its impact on developing countries.[6]

The present study focuses on the publication relating to gender issues in informatics on the basis of country wise analysis. In general bibliometric indicators play an important role in science policy decisions and in evaluation of researcher performance. It is observed that bibliometric indicators help to evaluate the research performance of individual scientists and research group. This study corresponds to analyze the extent of women engagement in the field of information technology on the basis of published output as a yardstick in different part of the world.[7]

This research is based on the published literature on the subject gender issue in informatics in the last two decades throughout the world. The outcome of the research includes an online database containing the total publication on gender issues in the area of informatics, an online thesaurus representing the themes discussed in the publications. A manual for the construction and use of the magic mapping in gender studies in computing and a state of art illustrating the results of research publications of the various countries on gender dimension in computing education and employment.

Now days publications are widely accepted as one of the indicators of the nature, direction, volume and characteristics of research as they collectively represent data relating to research efforts and scientific progress in that area. Such data over a period of time provide an understanding of the shifts and changing composition of a discipline. This study aims at analyzing the growth of literature on gender issues in informatics and it helps to analyze the knowledge structure in that field. Hence the major focus of this study is to collect the research outputs of the countries in the world on the areas of women in informatics and to produce cognitive maps. This study evaluates the research scenario of these countries with respect to women in information technology education, women in I.T. industry and gender gap in I.T. labour market and I.T. Education. The map highlights the strength and weakness of the research efforts through thematic mappings. These maps illustrate the research status of the individual countries, the most focused area of specialty (themes/issues),the most active countries in conducting research, and its impact of this research on gender development.[8]

This would benefit the academic researchers, policy planners, funding agencies and the professional associations and organizations. The resulting database of this work would be a ready reckoner for the researchers to decide upon their future areas of researches, while it helps them to avoid duplication of research efforts. This database could be used by planners for identifying the gender problems in information in order to device schemes for improving the situation. This type of studies give insight about monitoring numerical data, geometric properties of the data distribution, and searching for clusters and thereby become an intuitive and inspiring interactive process.

Further knowledge discovery in database is concerned with extracting useful information and data mining to be a single step in a large process.[9]

This study helps the conference organizers in the choice of the most vital themes for deliberations at various point of time and periodical conducting of seminars and conferences on women in informatics are the pre-requisition to get the essential input to the research. A constant interaction with the subject specialists would help to formulate the knowledge structure of the discipline gender in informatics and it would help to sharpen the domains, sub-domains and the foci of this subject that are essential in the construction of the thesaurus on this subject.

One could be aware of the knowledge sharing behaviours on the Gender Studies in Informatics. It helps to trace out the publications of authors, their affiliation, type of study, the type of data used, the nature of methodology, geographical coverage, institutional coverage, key words and an extended abstract that include the objectives, hypotheses and the findings.

This study explains the possible ways of constructing the magic mapping Gender Studies in Informatics. These mapping would help to find some important policy oriented issues, such as status of the individual countries in women in informatics, most focused area, distribution of research efforts, identification of major countries in the area of research and impact of information on gender development.

This study takes into account a wide research output in women in informatics. The study of institution wise growth rate and pattern of growth of literature on gender issues in informatics is considered to be an important attribute of scientometric analysis. Depending on the nature and content and identification of major countries in the area research and impact of information on gender development.

STATEMENT OF THE PROBLEM

This study attempts to examine the trend on gender issues in informatics. It aims at evaluating the research activity of the countries on gender issues in informatics, by means of their bibliographic out put. The last two decades have witnessed an overhelming volume of publications addressing the gender Issues in informatics. These studies have brought into lime light the contribution of scholars, researchers and academicians on this subject. This study attempts to explain the theoretical and empirical discussions relating to gender relations in informatics from the published reports. This analysis helps to identify the key issues affecting or favoring women in this field. Bibliometric techniques are employed to analyze the publications on gender studies to identify the trend in the publication, the thematic pattern etc.

Many of the publications have addressed the issue of passive participation of women in the informatics and its consequence on maintaining the gender equity in the society. Due to scattering of publications, the findings of this research have not been visible to the policy makers, who have been concerned with the gender disparity in the informatics education and employment. In order to overcome this problem, this study attempts to convert the publications into a comprehensive database. This would be a major step towards consolidating the research findings on one side and facilitating the visibility of the publications on the other. This database covers information relating to the authors and their affiliation; thematic coverage; methodology adopted and the institutional and regional coverage of the publications.

This study plans to analyse the growth of literature on the basis of growth rate analysis. The growth of literature on gender studies may vary from one country to another and from one continent to another. Hence this issue is taken into consideration in the present study. This study would indicate the research status of the countries on this subject, and identification of active research area and their impact of IT on gender development. This research would offer a base for integrating the corpus of these research outputs into the process of improving the curriculum, recruitment and retention activities in computing in order to create women friendly environment and also to encourage more women in all areas of education, employment and training in informatics.

This study takes into account the shortage of women in informatics education and the efforts being taken by the governments and IT employers of the world countries to achieve gender equity in informatics. The lack of participation of women in this sector would lead to serious socio-economic implications. This study plans to prepare cognitive map for evaluating the research scenario of the selected countries on the major subjects domains like women in I.T. Education, women in I.T. industry, gender gap in I.T. labour market and I.T. Education.

The analysis of sub-field in gender studies is informatics is one of the aspects of the present study. It traces out the potential areas and research-wise concentration in Gender Studies in Informatics. This type of analysis helps to identify the research gap in the previous studies.

OBJECTIVES

The following objectives are framed for the purpose of present study:

1. To examine the growth of literature in Gender Studies in Informatics during the period 1982-83 to 2002-2003.
2. To study the continent wise and country wise research output performance in Gender Studies in Informatics.
3. To analyse the cognitive structure of Gender Studies in Informatics and to identify changes, shifts during the period of study.
4. To examine the premier institutions, publishing the research output in gender studies at the global level.
5. To identify less productive and neglected areas of Gender Studies in Informatics.
6. To identify the nature of authorship pattern and determine the degree of collaboration.

2
Review of Literature

A comprehensive review of literature is a necessary integral part of any research, as it helps to identify the gap in research and aids the investigator in designing and analysing research work. Further, an acquaintance of earlier related studies is necessary to formulate appropriate research methodology. Keeping in mind the objectives set forth for the study, an attempt was made in this Chapter to review the available literature.

STUDIES RELATED TO MAPPING

Michelet Bertrand and Turner W.A.,[(1)] presented an initial version of the Co-word research system for document retrieval. The Keyword document indexing offer the possibility of detecting and changing the perception about the usefulness of words for scientific or technology activity. The source were French PASCAL CDST - CNRS Database which contained 3500 bibliographical references. Statistical coefficients were used to give an idea of the structural link that exists between the indexing words of a database.

Kostoff Ronald N., Fberhart, Henry J., and Toothman Darrell Ray[(2)] examined Database Tomography. They formed algorithms for extracting multi-word phrase frequencies and performing phrase proximity. They identified the technical themes and their relationships among technical themes and authors, journals, institutions and countries. They used DT methods in three steps. In the first step they identified the main themes of the text and secondly determined the quantitative and qualitative relationships among the main themes and their secondary themes and finally they tracked the evolution of these themes and their relationships through time.

Tijssen R.J.W., and Van Raan A.F.J[3] examined the LEXIMAPPE Method and multidimensional scaling. They discussed the methods visualizing the Characteristics of structured word-occurrence relation. They analyed in three preliminary steps namely (I) Determining word - linkage strengths (ii) Setting thresholds and (iii) introducing simplifications. They extended MDS map as a means to gain insight in both local and global structure. MDS is proposed as an alternative mapping method to circumvent problematic features of leximappe maps of the total co-words structure.

Tijssen, Robert J.W [4] Co-classification of energy research explains the basis of co-classification analysis. Co-Classification analysis is base on the network of inter disciplinary links between research fields. As manifest in the co-occurrence of different subset classification headings assigned to research publication. The database contains all types of publications irrespective of the source and language. Quantitative indicators derived from Co- classification analysis are a helpful element in describing and identifying features of multidisciplinary areas.

Noyons, E.C.M., and Can Raan, A.F.J [5] analyzed the tool to study the important aspects of the relation between science and technology. Cartographic approach was used to identify the research activity for development of products and for research institutes to identify possible application of knowledge. They investigated the science side and technology side of optomelhartronics and more specifically science as a basis for technology. Cartographic technique shows the observation of the structure of science and technology fields. They illustrated both existing as well as possible links between science and technology.

Tijssen, Robert J.W., and Vanraan, Anthony F.J[6] applied the phenomena of bibliometric co-occurrence for the pair solid-state physics. They applied multidimensional scaling based on a geometric distance. CO-word analysis involves co-occurrence of keywords given by authors, indexers or words extracted from publication titles or from their full text.

Courtial, J.P[7] analysed the nature of co-word analysis on selected scientific articles from PASCAL database belonging to scientometric studies for two time periods: 1988 - 1990 and 1992 - 93. Ten- word cluster were calculated. The network of clusters expresses the integrated development of the field around scientific research.

Lue Grivel, Peter Mutschke, Xavier Polanco[8] analysed on SDOC and classified the themes i.e., clusters of closely tied keywords, characterizing the domain study. In this study co-word analysis used SDOC method for identifying and visualizing the centers of interest in scientific literature. Key words are primarily used for information and retrieval by Boolean queries. The importance of a certain thematic aspects for the research field has been examined by considering clusters relationships in their internal structure and central role they play with in a network of themes.

Rikken ,F., kiers, H.A.L., and Vos, R[9] focussed on the problem of mapping the dynamics of Co-Word matrices from 1978-1990. The peripheral aspects are adverse drug reactions (ADR). The source was medical articles derived from the MEDLINE database. A matrix of Co-occurrence frequencies and a matrix of Jaccard. Co-efficient of all possible linkages between the words was constructed. They explored the possibilities of a three-way multi dimensional scaling method INDSCAL. The results imply that this study is useful for dynamics of co-word-matrices in a research field.

Cozzens,S.,[10] analyzed when U.S. congerss passed the Government performance and results Act (GPRA) in 1993 to improve the efficiency and effectiveness of federal programs by establishing a system of setting goals, for program performance and to measure results. Agencies with clear technological goals are rapidly developing sets of indicators for this use, including peer assessments, bibliometric measures including patents, and customer satisfaction rating, but fundamental research agencies do not find such measures satisfactory and are just beginning to develop alternative ones.

Planco, Xavier and Grivel,Luc.,[11] examined maps embedded in Bibliographical references by means of co-word analysis. It describes application of informetric chain to the social science information in the specific field of sociology. SDOC is an original implementation of co-word analysis. The co-word analysis has been broken down into the following steps: (1) Building keywords index from a set of reference (ii) Computing co-occurrences of keywords and measuring the similarity of the keywords (iii) Cutting up the keywords associations networks into clusters (iv) Classifying the references into clusters (v) Building scatter diagrams or maps. Here the co-word maps visualize the structure of relationships between subsets of research and the way in which this network evolves with time. This is useful to identify subset research areas and to investigate the distribution of publications, institutions, and countries in these areas of research.

Bhattacharya, Sujit[12] studied the techniques of activity Index and science strategy index. He analyzed the activity in physics over ten sub-fields as classified by IUPAP. Multi - dimensional scaling was applied on a similarity metric contracted using SSI. It allows to compare the structure of the publication output of countries. Multi-dimensional scaling helps to explore and infer the underlying structure.

Cabo, Pepin., and Boersma, Margreet.,[13] studied how keywords can be used for the study of technological innovation in Biotechnology. They studied how the innovation activity of public and private sector organizations can be compared, how degree of similarity can be computed and how differences can be qualified.

Ying Ding, Gobinda G. Chowdhury, Schubert Foo.,[14] mapped intellectual structure of the field of Information Retrieval (IR) during the period of 1987 -1997. Co -word analysis was employed to reveal patterns and trends in the IR field by measuring the association strengths of terms, representative of relevant publications or other texts produced in IR field. The results showed that the IR field has some established research themes and it also changes rapidly to embrace new themes.

Cronin Blaise.,[15] studied the social structure of women's studies and analysed all scholarly articles and acknowledgments appearing in three journals over a 20-year period. A content analysis was conducted of all editorial statements published by the journals. The results demonstrated the highly gendered nature of the field and the incompatibility of its stated objectives.

GROWTH ORIENTED STUDIES

Ramakrishna N.V.,[16] studied the growth of biotechnology literature. They tested exponential linear and logistic growth. Relative growth Rate (RGR) and Doubling Time (DT) were also applied to the study. The result showed that within equal economic, intellectual and environmental conditions, literature on different subjects follows similar growth trends.

Humayoon Kabir.,[17] analysed the bibliometric literature and found that the world literature on bibliometrics has been growing exponentially at a doubling rate of ten years since 1969. Team research was not popular among researchers in bibliometrics.

Maheswarappa B. S, and Ningoli M.H.,[18] tested the applicability of modified exponential logistic and lineer pattern in applied sciences. They result showed that the literature in applied science in India does not follow the exponential logistic and linear pattern.

Parvathamma, N and Gunjal, S.R.,[19] examined the rate of growth of Indian earth science literature. The results show that the mean relative growth rate has shown a declining trend from 0.35 during 1979-83 to 0.11 during 1984-88. Correspondingly, mean doubling time has increased from 2.6 years to 7 years for the same periods.

Preveen Sharma, and K.C Garg.,[20] examined 536 Papers published in journals and presented at conferences, symposium/seminars in the field of solar power. It is concluded that the Indian Scientists of this field publish their research findings in journals published from the scientifically advanced countries of the west.

Dhruv Raina, Gupta B.M, and Rohit Kandhari.,[21] identified the rate of growth of physics publications in India manifests close to a doubling behavior between 1905 and 1935, Which one of the saturation plateaus characteristics of the growth of any discipline begins to appear.

Ketty Rodriguez, and Moreiro JA.,[22] studied the growth and development of research in the field of ecology. The study assessed the growth pattern and the complexity of research in the field of ecology, from 1976-1993 in Spain and the five Spanish-speaking countries of the Caribbean. Results indicate that the growth of research in ecology is greater in spain.

Karki MMS., Garg KC., and Sharma praveen.,[23] investigated Indian organic chemistry research activity during 1971-1989 using chemical Abstracts. It attempts at quantification of national contribution to world efforts, identify areas of relative strengths and weakness and also models the growth of Indian organic chemistry output to world organic chemistry output as a whole and in sub-fields where the activity index for the world and India are similar.

AUTHORSHIP RELATED STUDIES

Gupta Davendra, K.,[24] analysed Librarianship literature on Ehtiopia. The result showed that more than 67percent of the Literature produced between 1967 and 1978. 30% of the literature are unauthorized items and 92 percent of the authored items are single authored items; 78 authors are responsible to produce 167 items, which on an average is about 2.2 items per authors.

Humayoon Kabir, S.,[25] studied the authorship pattern and the extent of research collaboration in the field of bibliometrics literature. The study revealed that solo research is more favorable than the collaborative research. The degree of collaboration is ranged between 0.20 and 0.35 during the period of study, with an overall average of 0.31.

Rana Madan, S and Agarwal, Sunita.,[26] studied the authorship and collaborative research patterns in Indian wildlife and fisheries. The proportion of single authored papers has decreased from 63.68 percent in 1980 to 52.74 percent in 1989. During the same period there was an increase in number of authors per paper from 1.57 in 1980 to 1.70 in 1989. The degree of collaboration also increased from 0.36 to 0.47.

G.Mahapatra and Bhagvan Das.,[27] examined the impact of research collaboration on growth of literature in geology during 1987to 1996. The result show that there is an increase in collaboration in Geology research and simultaneously a decrease in the amount of publications.

Garg, K.C. and Padhi, P.,[28] analysed 3174 papers published in journals in the field of laser science and technology. It indicated that only 401 papers were single authored and the rest 2773 were co-authored papers. Of the 2773 papers, only 687 were written in local domestic journals and others in internationally collaboration.

Macias-Chapula,Cesar A and Muangos-Nolasco Acacia.,[29] analysis AIDS documents as produced on sub-Saharan Africa. Results indicated a high pattern of collaboration through multiple authorship. Most documents were published in English 84.50 percent and French 14.73 percent. Over 57 percent corresponded to journal articles.

The study of authorship pattern is one of the important features of bibliometric analysis. In this context Maheswarappa, B.S., et al., [30] identified the authorship pattern in science and technology research output of Indian scientists. The results indicate the growing trends in multiple authorship.

Sridhar,M.S., [31] analysed the authorship pattern in space technology and identified the trends in authorship pattern. The result points out that collaborative research has got increasing attention on the part of the researchers. This is highlighted by the decline in number of single author contributed papers.

Gupta, D.K., [32] analysed the entomology literature of Nigeria during 1900-1973 with respect to authorship pattern. This study identified the trends in number of publications of papers in relation to authorship pattern. The result indicators that there has been declining in single author contributed papers in recent years.

Beaver, D.D., [33] made a bibliometric study on physics literature with a view to analyse the collaborative endeavour in physics research. The study identified the status of research in physics and output performance.

REFERENCES

1. **Michelet Bertrand** and **Turner W.A..**, "Co-word search: A system for information retrieval," ***Journal of information science***, 1985, pp.173-181.

2. **Kostoff Ronald N., Fberhart, Henry J.**, and **Toothman Darrell Ray.**, "Data Base Tomography for technical intelligence : A Road map of the near- earth space science and technology Literature," ***Information processing and management***, 34(1),1988,pp. 69-85.

3. **Tijssen R.J.W.**, and ***Van Raan A.F.J.***, "Mapping co-word structures: A comparison of multidimensional scaling and leximappe," ***Scientometrics***, 15(3-4), 1989, pp.283-295.

4. **Tijssen, Robert J.W.**, "A quantitative assessment of interdisciplinary structures in science and technology: co-classification analysis of energy research", ***Research policy***, 1992, pp. 27- 44.

5. **Noyons, E.C.M.**, and **Can Raan, A.F.J.**, "Bibliometric cartography of scientific and technological developments of an R&D field," ***Scientometrics***, 30(1), (1994) pp.157-173

6. **Tijssen, Robert J.W.**, and **Vanraan, Anthony F.J,.** "Mapping changes in S &T: Bibliomtric Co-occurrence analysis of the R&D Literature," ***Evaluation Review***, 18(1), 1994, pp. 98-115.

7. **Courtial, J.P.**, "A co-word analysis of scientometrics," 31(3), 1994, pp.251-260.

8. **Grivel, Lue., Mutschke, Peter., Polanco, Xavier** "Thematic Mapping on Bibliographical databases by cluster analysis: A description of the SDOC Environment with SOLIS," ***knowl.org***, 22(2), 1995.

9. **Rikken ,F., kiers, H.A.L.**, and **Vos, R.**, "Mapping the dynamics of adverse drug reactions in subsequent time periods," ***Scientometrics***, 33 (3), 1995, pp.367-380.

10. **Cozzens,S.**, "U.S.Research assessments : Recent developments, " ***Scientometrics***, 34(3), 1995, pp.351-362.

11. **Planco, Xavier** and **Grivel,Luc.**, "Mapping knowledge: The use of co-word analysis techniques for mapping a sociology data file of four publishing countries,"***JISSI***,1(2),1995.

12. **Bhattacharya, Sujit.**, "World structure of physics: A cross-national comparison," *JISSI*, 2(1), 1996.

13. **Cabo, Pepin.**, and **Boersma, Margreet.**, "A keyword analysis of joint biotechnology projects," *JISSI*, 1996

14. **Ying Ding, Gobinda G. Chowdhury, Schubert Foo.**, "Bibliography of information retrieval research by using co-word analysis," *Information Processing & Management*, 37, 2000, pp 817-842.

15. **Cronin Blaise.**, "Women's studies: Bibliometric and content analysis of the formative years," *Journal of documentation*, 53, 1997, pp.123-138.

16. **Ramakrishna N.V.**, "Bibliometrics of Animal Cell Culture Technology Literature; A Study Based on the Animal Cell Biotechnology," *Annals of Library Science and Documentation*, 46(3), 1991, pp.81-96.

17. **Humayoon Kabir.**, "World literature on bibliometrics: Authorship and Growth pattern," *ILA Bulletin*,18, 1993, pp.3-4.

18. **Maheswarappa B. S**, and **Ningoli M.H.**, "Growth of literature in the field of applied sciences in India (1965-89)," *INICAF*, 12, 1993, pp.192-200.

19. **Parvathamma, N** and **Gunjal, S.R.**, "Growth pattern of Literature and Scientific productivity of authors in Indian Earth Science 1978-88: A Bibliometric study", *Library Science*, 30(2), 1993, pp.54-63.

20. **Preveen Sharma**, and **K.C Garg.**, "Bibliometrics of Solar Power Research in India", *IASLIC Bulletin*, 38(4), 1993, pp.155-169.

21. **Dhruv Raina, Gupta B.M**, and **Rohit Kandhari.**, "Collaboration in Indian Physics: A case study of the Macro and Micro parametrization of sub-disciplines (1800-1950),"*Scientometrics*, 33(3),1995,pp.295-314.

22. **Ketty Rodriguez**, and **Moreiro JA.**, "Growth and Development of Research in the Field of Ecology; as Measured by Dissertation Title Analysis"; *Scientometrics*, 35(1), 1996, pp. 56-70.

23. **Karki MMS., Garg KC., and Sharma praveen**., "Activity and growth of organic chemistry in India during 1971-1989," *Scientometrics*, 49(2),2000,pp.278-278.

24. **Gupta Davendra, *K***., "Bibliometric study of literature on Ethiopian librarianship -1944-1992", ***Library Science***,31(4), 1994, pp.208-216.

25. **Humayoon Kabir, S**., "Authorship Trend and Solo Research in Bibliometrics: A Bibliometric study", ***Library Science***, 31(2), 1994, pp. 85-90.

26. **Rana Madan, S** and **Agarwal, Sunita**., "Authorship trends in India wildlife and fisheries literature - A bibliometric study", ***Annals of Library Science and Documentation***, 41(1), 1994, pp.13-18.

27. **G.Mahapatra and Bhagvan Das.,** "Impact of research collaboration on growth of literature in geology: A bibliometric study, ***SRELS Journal of information Management***, 37(2), 2000, pp.90-105.

28. **Garg, K.C.** and **Padhi, P.**, "A Study of Collaboration in Laser Science and Technology", ***Scientometrics***, 51(2), 2001, pp.415-427.

29. **Macias-Chapula,Cesar A** and **Muangos-Nolasco Acacia**.., "Bibliometric analysis of AIDS literature in Central Africa", ***Scientometrics***, 54(2), 2002, pp.309-317.

30. **Maheswarappa, B.S., et al.,** "Collaborative Research in Science and Technology: A Bibliometric Study," ***Journal of Library and Information Science***, Vol. 9, No. 2, 1984, pp. 154-159.

31. **Sridhar, M.S.,** "A Study of Co-authorship and Collaborative Research among Indian Space Technologists, R.D. Management ," Vol. 15, No. 3, 1985, pp. 231-237.

32. **Gupta, D.K.,** "Collaboration in Research Output: A Review and a Case Study of Collaborative Trends of Entomological Research in Nigeria," 1900-1973, INICAF, Vol. 1, No. 1, 1986, p. 57.

33. **Beaver, D.D.,** "Collaborative and Team Work in Physics," Czechoslovakia Journal of Physics, Vol., 36, 1986, p. 14.

3
Research Design

OBJECTIVES

This chapter deals with the hypothesis, methodological description, nature of sampling and method of data collection, description and relevance of statistical tools applied and limitations.

HYPOTHESES

The following hypotheses are formulated, keeping the content and coverage of the framed objectives.

1. There is a significant increase in the growth of literature during the period of study.
2. There is a significant inter continental and inter country variation in the growth and concentration of research output in Gender Studies in Informatics.
3. The cognitive structure of Gender Studies in Informatics varies significantly among the selected continents in the study.
4. There is a significant variation with respect to institutions, producing research output in Gender Studies in Informatics.

METHODOLOGY

This study aims at analyzing the trends in the development of Gender Studies in Informatics. This study traces out the past trends in the area of research in gender studies on the bases of cross section data. This study evaluates the contribution of countries to the growth pattern and development of research on this discipline during the last two decades. The aim is to build a comprehensive data base on women in informatics and to map the status of women in this discipline. This study in undertaken in two dimension. The first dimension relates to statistical analysis with respect to growth of literature, area wise research output, institution wise output source wise research output, country wise research output, authorship pattern, collaboration in research and so on. The second dimension relates to classification of documents into clusters and building scatter diagrams and maps. This study is partly exploratory and partly evaluatory in nature.

SAMPLING

Among the disciplines, the researcher has selected Gender Studies in Informatics. Many studies have highlighted gender issues in various dimensions and none of the studies concentrate on women's involvement in I.T.

DATA COLLECTION

The relevant data are obtained from various sources such as journal articles, conference proceedings, reports, projects, online discussion news items and so on. The relevant data are obtained from the abstracts and relevant data are down loaded from the online resources.

STATISTICAL TOOLS

(i) Co-efficient of Variation

In order to study the inequality in distribution of

literature, the Lorenz curve model is applied. Further inequality in the distribution of literature is studied with the help of coefficient variation model.

It is written as,

$$C.V = \frac{\sigma}{\bar{\chi}} \times 100$$

Where, C.V = Coefficient variation

σ = Mean

$\bar{\chi}$ = Standard deviation

ANOVA TWO WAY MODEL

In order to study the institution wise variation and subfield wise variation, the anova two way model is applied. It is written as,

Sources of Variation	*Sum of Squares*	*Degrees of Freedom*	*Mean Sum of Squares*	*Ratio of F*
Between Samples	SSC	(c – 1)	MSC = SSC/(c – 1)	MSC/MSE
Between Rows	SSR	(r – 1)	MSR = SSR/(r – 1)	MSR/MSE
Residual or Error	SSE	(c – 1) (r – 1)	MSE = SSE/(r – 1) (c – 1)	
Total	SST	n – 1		

SSC = Sum of Squares between Columns

SSR = Sum of Squares between Rows

SSE = Sum of Squares due to Error

SST = Total Sum of Squares

The sum of squares for the source 'Residual' was obtained by subtracting from the total sum of squares, the sum of squares between columns and rows, i.e.,

SSE = SST – (SSC + SSR)

The total number of degrees of freedom

= n – 1 or r – 1

Where c refers to number of columns, and r refers to number of rows,

Number of degrees of freedom between columns

= (c – 1)

Number of degrees of freedom between rows

= (r – 1)

Number of degrees of freedom for residual

= (c – 1) (r – 1)

The total sum of squares, sum of squares between columns and sum of squares between rows were obtained in the same way as before.

Residual or error sum of square = Total sum of squares – sum of squares between columns – sum of squares between rows.

The F values were calculated as follows:

$$F(\upsilon_1 \upsilon_2) = \frac{MSC}{MSE}$$

Where,

$\upsilon_1 = (c - 1)$ and $\upsilon_2 = (c - 1)(r - 1)$

$$F(\upsilon_1 \upsilon_2) = \frac{MSR}{MSE}$$

Where, $v_1 = (r - 1)$ and $v_2 = (c - 1)(r - 1)$

It is noted that the F value may not be the same in both cases, viz., and $v_1 = (c - 1)$ and $v_1 = (r - 1)$

The calculated values of F were compared with the table values and logical conclusions were drawn.

It would be clear from above that in problems involving two-way classification, 'Residual' is the measuring rod for testing significance. It represents the magnitude of variation due to forces called 'chance'.

RELATIVE GROWTH RATE

The relative growth rate is the increase in the number of publications/pages per unit of time. Here, one year is taken as the unit of time. The mean relative growth rate R (1-2) over a specified period of interval can be calculated from the following equation suggested by Mahapatra.

$$R(1-2) = \frac{W_2 - W_1}{T_2 - T_1}$$

Where,

R = Mean relative growth rate over the specific period of interval;

W_1 = log w_1 (Natural log of initial number of publications/ pages);

W_2 = log w_2 (Natural log of initial number of publications/pages);

$T_2 - T_1$ = The unit difference between the initial time and final time.

Therefore,

R (a) = Relative growth rate per unit of publications per unit of time (year)

R (P) = Relative growth rate per unit of pages per unit of time (year)

DOUBLING TIME

A direct equivalence exists between the relative growth rate and doubling time. If the number of publications/pages of a subject doubles during a given period, then the difference between the logarithms of the numbers at the beginning and at the end of the period must be the logarithms of the number 2. This difference has a value of 0.693. Thus, the corresponding doubling time for publication and pages can be calculated by the following formula:

$$\text{Doubling time (Dt)} = \frac{0.693}{\bar{R}}$$

Therefore,

$$\text{Doubling time for publications Dt (a)} = \frac{0.693}{\bar{R}(a)}$$

ACTIVITY INDEX

The proportion of the contribution of a country is seen from two different angles eventhough both analyze the productivity of a country in terms of growth. i.e., (i) volume of papers produced by a country in different years and thus the extent of increase; and (ii) volume of growth in different years in relation to the world productivity.

To gauge the productivity, the performance index is applied in the study.

$$PI = \left\{\frac{CAO/Yr}{AOC/Yr}\right\} \times 100$$

PI = Performance Index

CAO = Country's Average Output

AOC = Average Output of Continent

Yr = Total years of the study period

The performance index is used to measure the productivity of a country in relation to the continent output. The activity index of a country is measured by:

A similar performance index is constructed to analyze the relative position of the country at the world level. The performance index is constructed as follows:

$$PI = \left\{\frac{CAO/Yr}{WAO/Yr}\right\} \times 100$$

PI = Performance Index

CAO = Country's Average Output

WAO = World Average Output

Yr = Total years of the study period

COWORD METHOD

Coword method is one of the tools of scientometrics. Articles from journals related to the study area collected for last two decades. Keywords used to describe the contents of an article which are the basic building blocks of a research field structure. A cluster of keywords can be understood as a short description of a research theme. A research field is then described as a structure of mutually connected research themes.

A research theme can be identified by using the information about common occurrences of keywords in some articles. Let's calculate an association index as:

$$e_{ij} = f_{ij}^{2} / (f_i f_j)$$

Where, f_{ij} is the number of common presence of keywords i and j in an article, f_i is the total number of occurrences of the world i in all the articles can understand an association index as a measure of strength of ties between keywords in a research field. This measure is then used for clustering the key words into research themes.

Each research theme obtained in this process has two parameters. The first one, called density measures the strength of internal ties among all keywords describing the research theme. We can understand this parameter as a measure of the theme development. The second one, called centrality, measures the strength of external ties to other themes. We can understand this parameter as a measure of importance of a theme in the development of the entire analyzed field.

Both median and mean values for density and centrality can be used in classifying themes into four groups.

Thereafter, a research field can be understood as a set of research themes, mapped in a strategic diagram - graph made by plotting themes according to their centrality and density rank values or values along two axes, x- are centality, y-axe density. Strategic diagrams with rank values are used more commonly than the ones with values, because of their legibility.

Themes in the first quadrant are both well developed and important for the structuring of a research field. Themes in the fourth quadrant have well developed internal ties but unimportant external ties and so are only of a marginal importance for the field. Themes in the third quadrant are both weekly developed and marginal themes in the second quadrant are important for a research field but are not developed. This study use the clock wise convention of quadrant numbering and we hope it won't cause any misunderstandings later in the text.

In this paper, a strategic diagram and its changes over periods of time are the main tools for the analysis of dynamics of the artificial neural networks field.

DEGREE OF COLLABORATION

The degree of collaboration is defined as the ratio of the number of collaborative research papers to the total number of research papers in the discipline during a certain period of time. The formula suggested by Subramanyam is used. It is expressed as:

$$C = \frac{Nm}{Nm + Ns}$$

Where, C is the degree of collaboration in a discipline. Nm is the number of multi-authored research papers in the discipline published during a year. Ns is the number of single authored papers in the discipline published during the same year. Using this formula the degree of collaboration is determined.

CONCEPTS

Scientometries

Quantitative analysis of bibliographic data of scientific publications with the objective to find characteristics of research performance.

Mapping Techniques

Mappings are constructed to see the growth of research output in the area of Gender Studies in Informatics.

Gender Studies

It explains the research studies conducted through out the globe pertaining to of women's education in information technology, and income and employment generation through Information Technology.

Cognitive structure

It explains the development of area wise research output in Gender Studies in Informatics, institution wise research performance and co classification analysis of subjects.

Limitations

The findings of this apply only to Gender Studies in Informatics and it does not apply to other fields. This study covers gender issues only with respect to women's I.T. Education and income and employment generation through information technology and other aspects of women development programmer are not brought under the purview of the study, because studying of all aspects of women development is not possible by the level of an individual researcher, due to constraints imposed by money, time, energy and efforts. This study does not take into account citations and their impacts, key word analysis, since it is a new area of research, This study is pursued with certain degree of caution.

4
Results and Discussions

Table 1. Distribution of Source wise Publication of Research Output

Source	No. of Publication	Percentage
Conference Proceedings	479	45.84
Journal Articles	349	33.39
News Item	111	10.62
Project Publication	44	4.21
Online Publication	62	5.94
Total	1045	100.00

Source: Online Resources

Data presented in table 1 indicates the source-wise publication of research output in Gender Studies in Informatics between 1982-83 and 2002-03. It could be noted that out of the total 1045 publications, conference proceedings form of publication constitutes 45.84 per cent of the total publications. Journal articles form of publication constitute 33.39 per cent during the study period.

Out of the total 1045 publications, 10.62 per cent of them are in the form of news item and 4.21 per cent of them are in the form of project report. Moreover, 5.94 per cent of them are available in the form of online publications.

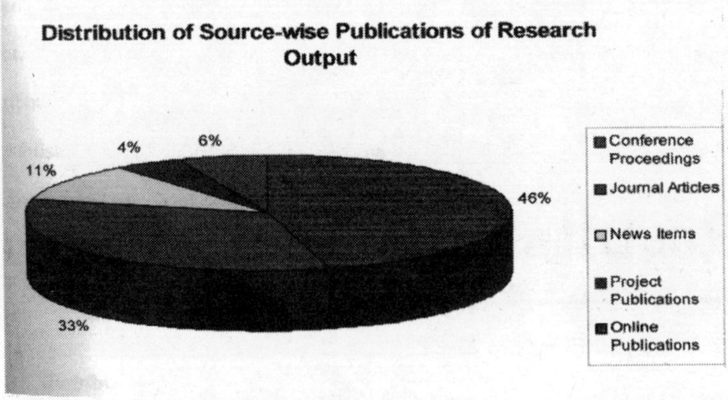

It could be Seen clearly from the above discussion that the Conference proceedings form of research output in Gender Studies in Informatics occupy the first order of reporting, journal article form the second, news item the third, online publications the fourth and project report form of publications the last.

Table 2. Distribution of Continent-wise Research Output in Gender Studies in Informatics

Continent	No. of Output	Percentage
Africa	52	4.97
Asia	98	9.38
Australia	24	2.29
Europe	228	21.83
North America	643	61.54
Total	1045	100.00

Source: Online Resources

A study of data in table 2 indicates the continent-wise publication of literature in Gender Studies in Informatics. It could be seen that out of the total 1045 research output, 4.97 per cent of them are published in Africa and 9.38 per cent of them are contributed by Asian scholars. Of the total 045 research output, 2.29 per cent of them are published by Australian scholars and 21.83 per cent of them are published by European scholars. It is interesting to note that more than a three-fourth of the (83.37%) publications belong to the North American and European continents.

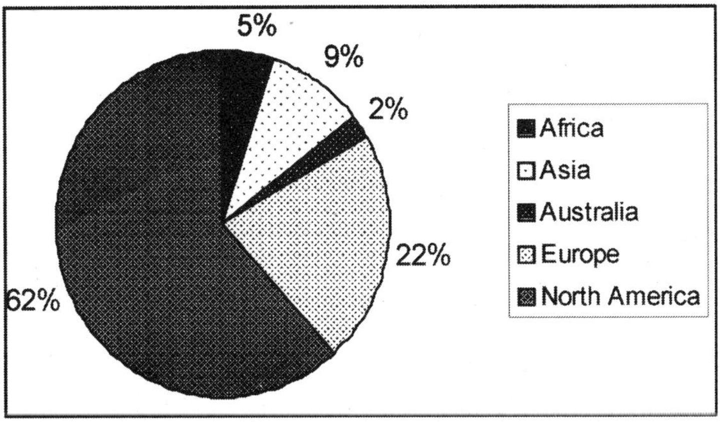

Chart 2. Distribution of Continent-wise Research Output in Gender Studies in Informatics

It could be seen clearly from the above discussion that the North American continent has contributed highest number of research output in Gender Studies in Informatics and Australia takes the lowest position in contribution of research output. European continent takes the second place in order with respect to research output contribution in Gender Studies in Informatics, Asia the third and Africa the fourth.

Data presented in table 3 indicate the continent-wise sources of publication of research output in Gender Studies in Informatics. It could be noted that in the African continent journal form (36.54%) and online discussion (30.77%) form of publications occupy the predominant position with respect to overall publication of research output in Gender Studies in Informatics. In the Asian continent more than a two-third of the publications are conference proceedings (70.41%). In the Australian continent, more than three-fourths of the publications are either conference proceedings (45.83%) or journal articles (37.5%). In the European continent, more than a half of the publications (52.63%) are in the form of conference proceedings. In the North American continent conference proceedings (41.52%) and journal articles (37.64%) occupy the predominant positions.

Table 3. Continent-wise Distribution of Publication of Research Output in Gender Studies in Informatics

Country	Conference Proceedings	Journal Article	News Item	Project	Online Discussion	Total
Africa	12 (23.08)	19 (36.54)	4 (7.69)	1 (1.92)	16 (30.77)	52 (100)
Asia	69 (70.41)	8 (8.16)	4 (4.08)	3 (3.06)	14 (14.29)	98 (100)
Australia	11 (45.83)	9 (37.5)	3 (12.5)	-	1 (4.17)	24 (100)
Europe	120 (52.63)	71 (31.14)	19 (8.33)	11 (4.82)	7 (3.07)	228 (100)
North America	267 (41.52)	242 (37.64)	81 (12.6)	29 (4.51)	24 (3.73)	643 (100)
Total	479 (45.84)	349 (33.4)	111 (10.62)	44 (4.210)	62 (5.93)	1045 (100)

Source: Online Resources

Figures in parentheses denote percentage

It could be seen clearly from the above discussion that in the African continent conference proceedings form of publication are less than other continents. The journal articles form of publication is predominant in Asian and European continents and conference proceedings cum journal article form of publications of Gender Studies in Informatics in Australian and North American continents.

Data presented in table 4 indicate the country-wise research output in Gender Studies in Informatics in the African continent. In this continent, 12 conference

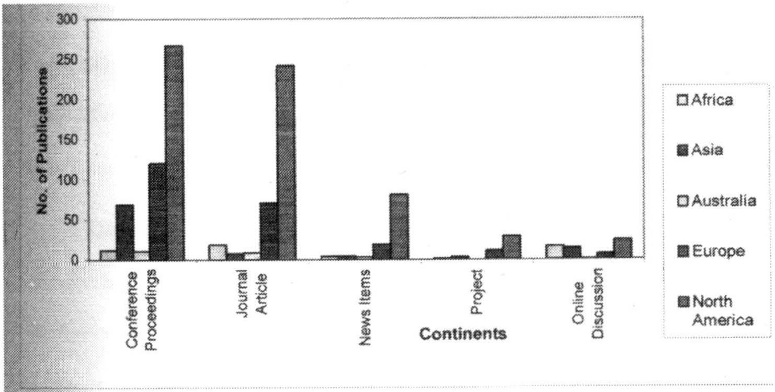

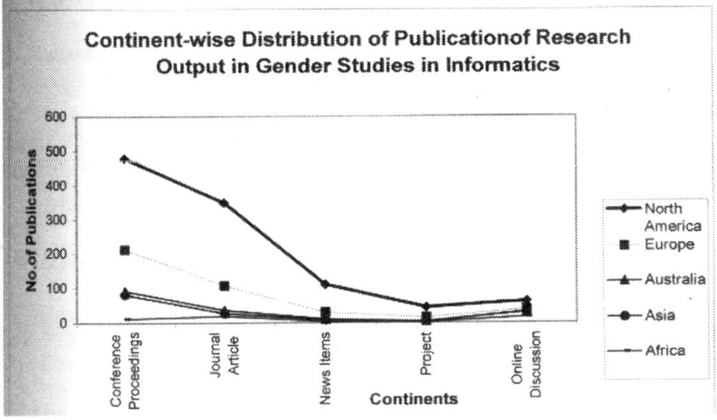

Chart 3. Continent-wise Distribution of Publication of Research Output in Gender Studies in Informatics

proceedings form of research output in Gender Studies in Informatics and 19 of them are in the form of journal article during the stud) period. This form of publication is mainly observed in Nigeria (50%). This type of publication is also seen Ghaha, Mauritus, Sierra Leone, South Africa and Tanzania.

Out of the total publications in African continent, 19 (36.54%) are in the form of journal articles. They are mostly contributed from South Africa (94.24%) and (5.26%) Nigeria.

It is noted that the journal form of publication has not received attention in the remaining thirteen countries. Of the total 52 publications in the South African continent, 4 (7.69%) of them are in the form of news item. This type of publication is observed each one in Burkina Faso South Africa, Tanzania and Uganda. Only one project form of publication is reported in the African continent that too only in South Africa.

Table 4. Country-wise Source of Publication of Research Output in Gender Studies in Informatics in African Continent

Country	Conference rocee-dings	'Journal Articles	News Item	Projects	Online Discus-sions	Total
Burkina Faso	-	-	1 (25)	-	-	1 (1.92)
Ghana	1 (8.33)	-	-	-	-	1 (1.92)
Malawi	-	-	-	-	2 (14.8)	2 (3.85)
Mali	-	-	-	-	1 (7,14)	1 (2.00)
Mauritius	1 (8.33)	-	-	-	-	1 (2.00)
Morocco	-	-	-	-	1 (7.14)	1 (2.00)
Nigeria	6 (50)	1 (5.26)	-	-	1 (7.14)	8 (16.00)
Sierra Leone	1 (8.33)	-	-	-	-	1 (2.00)
South Africa	2 (16.67)	18 (94.74)	1 (25)	1 (100)	3 (21.42)	25 (50.00)
Tanzania	1 (8.33)	-	1 (25)	-	-	2 (4.00)
Tunisia	-	-	-	-	2 (14.8)	2 (4.00)

Uganda	-	-	1 (25)	-	1 (7.14)	1 (2.00)
Zambia	-	-	-	-	1 (7.14)	1 (2.00)
Zimbabwe	-	-	-	-	2 (14.8)	2 (4.00)
Total	12 (24.00)	19 (38.00)	4 (8.00)	1 (2.00)	14 (28.00)	50 (100)

Source: Online Resources

Figures in parentheses denote percentage

Of the total 50 publications, 14(28.00%) of them are in the form of online discussion, South Africa has more number (21.42%) of such publications than the other nine countries that publish this type of research output. Online discussion form of publications have not been reported in any of the five countries in the African continent.

It could be seen clearly from the above discussion that South Africa tops the list among the countries in the African continent in publishing research output in Gender Studies in Informatics. Nigeria comes next in position. In this study six countries each published only two papers and seven countries each published only one paper during the study period. South Africa alone has all sources of published research output.

A study of data in table 5 indicates the country-wise sources of publication of research output in Gender Studies in Informatics in the Asian continent. This continent has 68 conference proceeding form of publications and most of them (95.65%) are published by Indian scholars. Japan and Singapore each one has published one conference proceeding form of research output in Gender Studies in Informatics. Of the 8 (8.16%) journal article form of publications, Bangladesh and India each share 25 per cent of the publications. Further, Indonesia, Japan, Malaysia and Philippines each one has published one journal article form of research output. Five countries have not contributed any paper in this regard. This study has 3 (3.12%) news item form of research output in Gender Studies in Informatics and it is published by two countries viz., India (66.6%), and Thailand (33.3%). Further, seven countries have not published any paper in this regard.

Table 5. Country-wise Distribution of Publication of Research Output in Gender Studies in Informatics in the Asian Continent

Country	Conference Procee-dings	Journal Articles	News Item	Projects	Online Discus-sions	Total
Bangladesh	-	2 (25)	-	-	-	2 (2.08)
India	66 (95.65)	2 (25)	2 (66.6)	-	2 (14.29)	72 (75.00)
Indonesia	-	1 (12.5)	-	-	1 (7.14)	2 (2.08)
Japan	1 (1.47)	1 (12.5)	-	-	-	2 (2.08)
Malaysia		1 (12.5)	-		-	1 (1.04)
Philippines	-	1 (12.5)	0	1 (33.33)	8 (57.14)	10 (10.4)
Singapore	1 (1.47)		-	-	-	1 (1-04)
South Korea	-	-	-	1 (33.33)	2 (14.29)	3 (3.12)
Sri Lanka	-	-	-	1 (33.33)	2 (7.14)	2 (2.08)
Thailand	-	-	1 (33.3)	-		1 (1.04)
Total	68 (70.8)	8 (8.33)	3 (3.12)	3 (3.12)	14 (14.58)	96 (100)

Source: Online Resources

Figures in parentheses denote percentage

It is seen that 3 (3.06%) project form of research output are published in the Asian continent. They are published from Philippines, South Korea and Sri Lanka, each one. This study has 14 online discussion form of publications. They are published by scholars of five countries, viz., Philippines (57.14%), India (14.29%), South Korea (14.29%), Sri Lanka (7.14%) and Indonesia (7.14%).

It could be seen clearly from the above discussion that seven countries have not published conference proceeding form of research output in Asian continent. Most of the publications are brought out by Indian scholars. Five countries have not published any paper in journal article form. Among the countries the contribution of India and Bangladesh are the noteworthy. Eighth countries have not published any paper in the form of news item. It is published by two countries viz., India, and Thailand. Eight countries have not published any paper in the form of project and it is reported only two countries. Further, five countries have not published any paper in the form of online discussion.

Table 6 presents data on the country-wise sources of research output in Gender Studies in Informatics. It could be noted that out of the total 230 research output in European continent, 52.63 per cent of them are published in the form of conference proceedings. England tops the list (62.80%) in publishing more number of conferences proceeding form of publications. The Netherlands takes the next position (9.09%), Germany (6.61%) and Ireland (5.78%) the third. Three countries have 2 papers each and two countries have each 3 paper publications in the form of conference proceedings in Gender Studies in Informatics. Further, six countries have each one publication.

Of the total 230 publications in the European continent, 30.86 per cent of them are in the form of journal articles. Here also, England occupies a predominant position (77.46%). The Netherlands comes next (4.23%), two countries have each 2 paper publications and seven countries have each 1 publication in the form of journal article.

Table 6. Country-wise Source of Publication of Research Output in Gender Studies in Informatics in the European Continent

Country	Conference Procee-dings	Journal Articles	News Item	Projects	Online Discus-sions	Total
Austria	2 (1.65)	1 (1.41)	-	-	-	3 (1-30)
England	76 (62.80)	55 (77.46)	15 (75.00)	8 (72.73)	4 (57.14)	158 (68.69)
Bulgaria	1 (0,82)	1 (141)	-	-	-	2 (0.86)
Croatia	-	-	-	-	2 (28.57)	2 (0.86)
Denmark	1 (0.82)	2 (2.82)	-	-	-	3 (130)
Finland	3 (2.47)	-	-	-	-	3 (1-30)
France	2 (1.65)	1 (1.41)	1 (5.00)	1 (9.09)	1 (14.29)	6 (2.60)
Switzerland	-	2 (2.82)	-	1 (9.09)	-	3 (1.30)
Germany	8 (6.61)	-	-	-	-	8 (3-47)
Ireland	7 (5.78)	1 (1-41)	1 (5.00)	-	-	9 (3.91)
Italy	1 (0.82)	-	-	-	-	1 (0.43)
Jordan	1 (0.82)	-	-	-	-	1 (0.43)
Israel	1 (0.82)	-	1 (5.00)	-	-	2 (0.86)
Norway	2 (1.67)	1 (1.41)	-	-	-	3 (1-30)

Russia	1 (0.82)	2 (2.82)	-	-	-	3 (1.30)
Scotland	3 (2.47)	1 (1.41)	-	1 (9.09)	-	5 (2.17)
Sweden	1 (0.82)	1 (1.41)	-	-	-	2 (0.86)
The Netherlands	11 (9.09)	3 (4.23)	2 (10.00)	-	-	16 (6.95)
Total	121 (52.60)	71 (30.86)	20 (8.69)	11 (4.78)	7 (3.04)	230 (100)

Source: Online resources

Figures in parentheses denote percentage

Out of the total 230 research output in the European continent, 8.69 per cent of them are in the form of news item. This form of publications is observed only in four countries of which England tops the list (57.14%). In this analysis, 4.78 per cent of the publications are in the form of project report. Project form of publication is observed in four countries of which England tops the list. In the European continent 3.04 per cent of them are published in the form of online discussion. This form of publication is found in three countries and England is the major contributor.

It could be seen clearly from the above discussion that England shares more than two-thirds of the publications in Europe. The Netherlands contributes a considerable level of publications. The remaining sixteen countries share less than 25 per cent of the total output in the European continent. It could be noted that fifteen countries have not published any paper in the form of online discussion and fourteen countries in the form of project or news item form of publications.

Table 7 presents the country-wise distribution of research output in Gender Studies in Informatics. It could be noted that out of the total 24 publications, 45.83 percent of them are in the form of conference proceedings and they are published only in Australia. Of the total 24 publications,

37.5 per cent of them are in the form of journal articles and most of them are published in Australia. The Australian continent has 3 news item forms of publications and all of them are published in Australia and it has only one online discussion form of publication which is published only in New Zealand.

Table 7. Country-wise Distribution of Publication of Research Output in Gender Studies in Informatics in the Australian Continent

Country	Conference Procee-dings	Journal Articles	News Item	Projects	Online Discus-sions	Total
Australia	11 (100.00)	8 (88.84)	3 (10.00)	-	-	22
New Zealand	-	1 (11.11)	-	-	1 (100.00)	2
Total	11 (45.83)	9 (37.5)	3 (12.5)	-	1 (4.17)	24 (100)

Source: Online Resources

Figures in parentheses denote percentage

It could be seen clearly from the above discussion that Australia shares most of the publications in the Australian continent and New Zealand shares only 2 publications of research output in Gender Studies in Informatics.

A study of data in table 8 indicates the country-wise source of research output in Gender Studies in Informatics in the North American continent. In this continent, nine countries have contributed their research output. It could be noted that out of the total 645 papers published in the North American continent, 41.39 per cent of them are in the form of conference proceedings. They are mostly published in Canada (55.05%) and USA (44.19%).

Of the total 645 publications in the North American continent, 37.52 per cent of them are in the form of journal article. They are mostly published in USA (98.76%) and the rest of them are published in Canada (1.23%). Out of the total 645 papers published in the North American continent, most of them news item are published in USA (97.53%) and the rest of them are published by Canadian scholars (2.47%). All the project form of publication are contributed by American scholars. Out of the total 645 publications, 4.03 per cent of them are in the form of online discussions and most of them are (80.76%) contributed by American scholars and the rest of them by scholars of Central America (7.69%) and Gautemala (3.84%).

Table 8. Country-wise Source of Publication of Research Output in Gender Studies in Informatics in the American Continent

Country	Conference Procee-dings	Journal Articles	News Item	Projects	Online Discus-sions	Total
Canada	147 (55.05)	3 (1.23)	2 (2.47)	-	-	152 (23.56)
Central America	-	-	-	-	2 (7.69)	2 (0.31)
Guatemala	-	-	-	-	1 (3.84)	1 (0-15)
Mexico	2 (0.75)	-	-	-	-	2 (0.31)
USA	118 (44.19)	239 (98.76)	79 (97.53)	29 (100)	21 (80.76)	486 (75.34)
Argentina	-	-	-	-	2 (7.69)	2 (0.31)
Total	267 (41.39)	242 (37.52)	81 (12.5)	29 (4.49)	26 (4.03)	645 (100)

Source: Online Resources Figures in parentheses denote percentage

It could be seen clearly from the above discussion that USA is the leader contributor in research output in Gender Studies in Informatics. Canada shares

A considerable level of research output in Gender studies in Informatics and the contribution of other countries is quite discouraging as they have less than one per cent each.

Table 9. Relative Growth Rate of Overall Output in Gender Studies in Informatics

Year	Total Output	Cumu-lative		w2	R(a)	Mean (a) 1-2	Doubling Time	Mean pt (a) 1-2
1982-83	2	2	-	0.693	-			
1984-85	1	3	0.693	1.09	0.397		1.74	
1986-87	3	6	1.09	1.79	0.70		0.99	
1988-89	30	36	1.79	3.58	1.79		0.38	
1990-91	61	97	3.58	4.57	0.99		0.70	
1992-93	29	126	4.57	4.83	0.26	0.82	2.66	1.29
1994-95	60	186	4.83	5.23	0.40		1.73	
1996-97	134	320	5.23	5.76	0.53		1.30	
1998-99	213	533	5.76	6.27	0.51		1.35	
2000-01	212	745	6.27	6.61	0.34		2.03	
2002-03	300	1045	6.61	6.95	0.34	0.36	2.03	1.40
Total						0.26		1.35

Source: Online Resources

A study of data in table 9 indicates the relative growth rate of research output in Gender Studies in Informatics at the global level. It is apparent that the relative growth rate has trend or more or less similar trend 0.39 in 1982-83 to 0.34 in 2002-2003. The mean relative growth rate for the period 1982-83 and 1992-93 is worked out to 0.82 and it is 0.36 for the period 1994-95 and 2002-2003. The overall study period has witnessed a mean relative growth rate of 0.26. Invariably the doubling time for publications of research output in gender studies has increased from 1.74 years in 1984-85 to 2.03 in 2002-2003. Quite obviously the whole study period has recorded a mean doubling time for publication as 1.35 years. The mean doubling time for the period 1982-83 to 1992-

Chart – 4

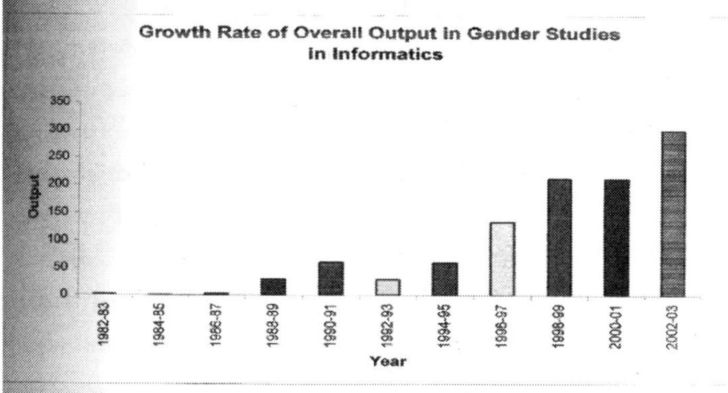

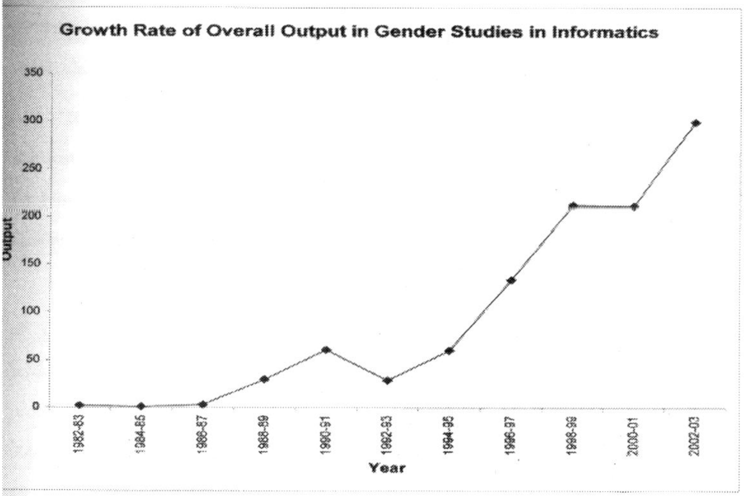

93 is worked out to 1.29 years and for the period 1994-95 to 2002-2003 it is calculated as 1.40 years.

It is evident from the above discussion that the relative growth rate of publication has shown more or less a similar trend. Consequently, the mean doubling time for publication of Gender Studies in Informatics has shown an increasing trend.

A keen observation of data in table 10 indicates the

relative growth rate of conference proceeding form of publications in Gender Studies in Informatics. It could be observed that the relative growth rate of conference proceedings form of research output has decreased from 1.09 in 1986-87 to 0.44 in 2002-2003. The mean relative growth rate for the period 1986-87 to 1992-93 is worked out to 0.90 and it is 1.65 for the period 1997-95 to 2002-03.

Table 10. Relative Growth Rate of Conference Proceedings Form of Research Output in Gender Studies in Informatics

Year	Total Output	Cumulative		w2	R(a)	Mean (a) 1-2	Doubling Time	Mean pt (a) 1-2
1982-83	1 .	1	-	0	-	-	-	
1984-85	0	1	0	0	-	-	-	
1986-87	2	3	0	1.09	1.09	-	63.58	
1988-89	23	26	1.09	3.26	2.17		0.32	
1990-91	53	79	3.26	4.37	1.11		0.62	
1992-93	13	92	4.37	4.52	0.15	0.904	4.62	17.29
1994-95	40	132	4.52	4.88	0.36		1.93	
1996-97	88	220	4.88	5.39	0.51		1.36	
1998-99	40	260	5.39	5.56	0.17		4.08	
2000-01	47	307	5.56	5.73	0.17		4.08	
2002-03	172	479	5.73	6.17	0.44	1.65	1.58	2.606
Total	479					0.617		9.13

Source: Online Resources

The overall study period has witnessed a mean relative growth rate of 0.617. Significantly, the doubling time for conference proceeding of the research output in gender studies has decreased from 63.58 years in 1986-87 to 1.58 years in 2002-2003. Thus is due to rapid increase is research publications from 2000-01 to 2002-03. The mean doubling time for the period 1986-87 to 1992- 93 is worked out to 17.29 years and it is 2.606 years for the period 1994-95 to 2002-03.

The whole study period has witnessed the mean doubling time for conference proceeding form of publication as 9.13 years.

Chart – 5

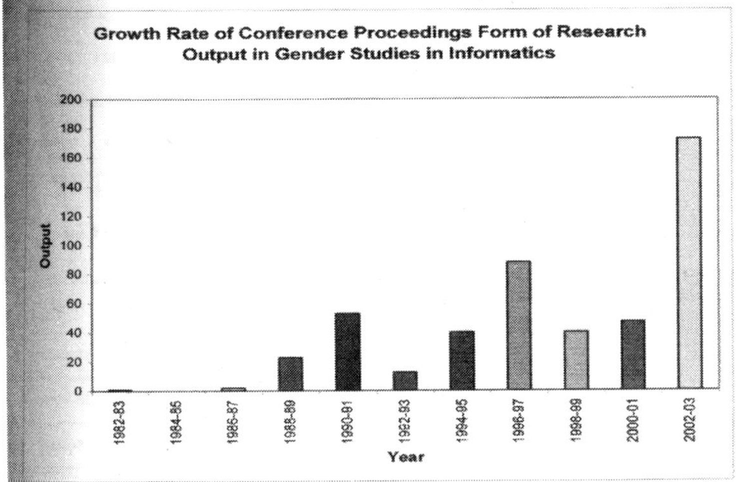

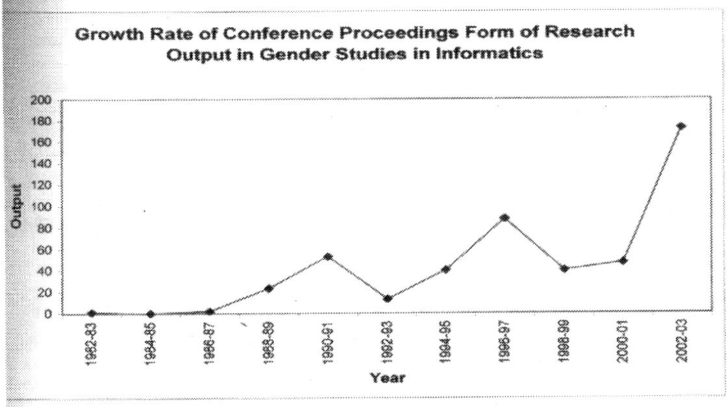

It could be deduced from the above discussion that the mean relative growth rate of conference proceeding form of publication has shown a declining trend. Consequently the mean doubling time for publication has also shown a declining trend, due to rapid increase in output during 2000-01 and 2002-03.

Table 11. Relative Growth Rate of Journal Article Form of Publications in Gender Studies in Informatics

Year	Total Output	Cumu-lative		w2	R(a)	Mean (a) 1-2	Doubling Time	Mean pt (a) 1-2
1982-83	1	1	-	0	-	-	-	
1984-85	1	2	0	0.693	0.693	-	1	
1986-87	1	3	0.693	1.1	0.407		1.7	
1988-89	7	10	1.1	2.3	1.2		0.58	
1990-91	8	18	2.3	2.89	0.59		1.17	
1992-93	15	33	2.89	3.5	0.61	0.7	1.14	1.12
1994-95	19	52	3.5	3.95	0.45		1.54	
1996-97	29	81	3.95	4.39	0.44		1.58	
1998-99	72	153	4.39	5.03	0.64		1.08	
2000-01	123	276	5.03	5.62	0.59		1.17	
2002-03	73	349	5.62	5.86	0.24	0.472	2.89	1.65
Total	349					0.59		1.39

Source: Online Resources

Data presented in table 11 indicate the relative growth rate of journal article form of research output in Gender Studies in Informatics. It could be noted that the relative growth rate has decreased from 0.693 in 1984-85 to 0.24 in 2002-03. The years 1988-89 and 1998-99 are out of trend due to manifold increase in journal form of output in Gender Studies in Informatics than in the other years. The mean relative growth rate for the period 1984-85 to 1992-93 is worked out to 0.7 and for the period 1994-95 to 2002-03 it is 0.47. The whole study period has witnessed a mean relative growth rate of 0.59.

Contrastingly, the doubling time for journal article

Chart – 6

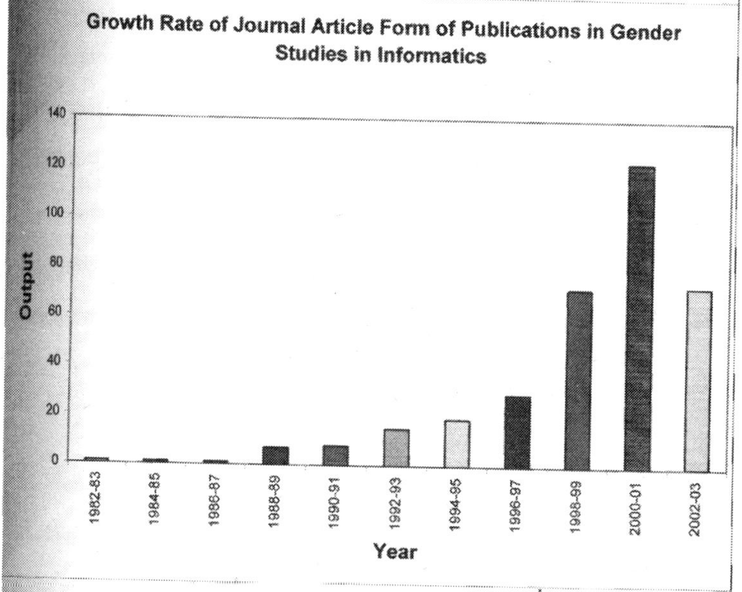
Growth Rate of Journal Article Form of Publications in Gender Studies in Informatics
Output
Year
0
20
40
60
80
100
120
140
1982-83
1984-85
1986-87
1988-89
1990-91
1992-93
1994-95
1996-97
1998-99
2000-01
2002-03

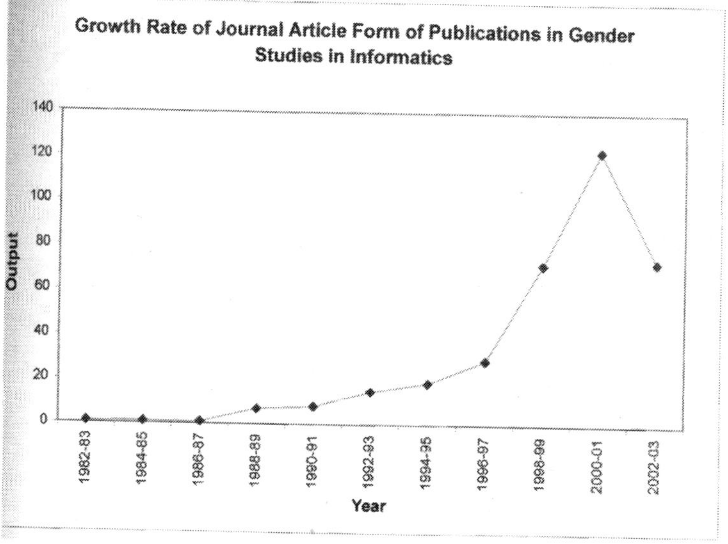
Growth Rate of Journal Article Form of Publications in Gender Studies in Informatics
Output
Year
0
20
40
60
80
100
120
140
1982-83
1984-85
1986-87
1988-89
1990-91
1992-93
1994-95
1996-97
1998-99
2000-01
2002-03

form of publications has increased from 1 year in 1984-85 to 2.89 years in 2002-03. The decline in doubling time in 1988-89 is due to a massive level of increase in journal article form of output during the year. The mean doubling time publications for the period 1984-85 is 1.12 years and it is 1.65 years for the period 1986-87 to 2002-03. The whole period has witnessed a mean doubling time of publication as 1.39 years.

It could be deduced from the above discussion that though the relative growth rate has shown a declining trend it has shown an increasing trend during 1984-85 and 1992-93. Contrastingly, the doubling time for publication has shown an increasing trend in journal article form of publications.

Table 12. Relative Growth Rate of News Item Form of Publications

Year	Total Output	Cumulative		w2	R(a)	Mean (a) 1-2	Doubling Time	Mean pt (a) 1-2
1992-93	1	1	-	0	-	-	-	
1994-95	1	2	0	0.693	0.693	#	1	
1996-97	5	7	0.693	1.95	1.257	-	0.55	
1998-99	16	23	1.95	3.14	1.19	-	0.58	
2000-01	35	58	3.14	4.06	0.92	-	0.75	
2002-03	53	111	4.06	4.71	0.65	0.942	1.07	0.79
Total	111	-						

Source: Online Resources

A study of data in table 12 indicates the relative growth rate of news item form of publications in Gender Studies in Informatics. It could be noted that the relative growth rate of news item form of publication in gender studies has decreased from 0.693 in 1994-95 to 0.65 in 2002-03. However, the mean relative growth rate for the period 1992-93 in 2002-

03 has shown an increasing trend and it is worked out to 0.94. This is due to a progressive increase in its publication in 1996-97, and 1998-99 than in the other years.

The doubling time for publication of news item form has increased from 1 year in 1994-95 to 1.07 year in 2002-03. However, the mean doubling time for publication has shown a declining trend, indicating a rapid increase in the form of publication during the period of analysis.

Chart – 7

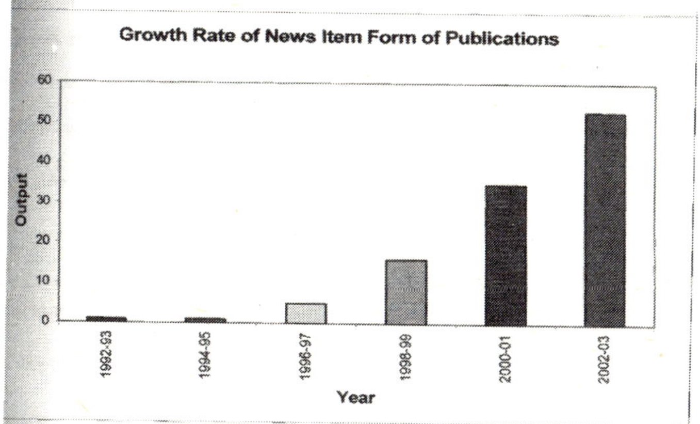

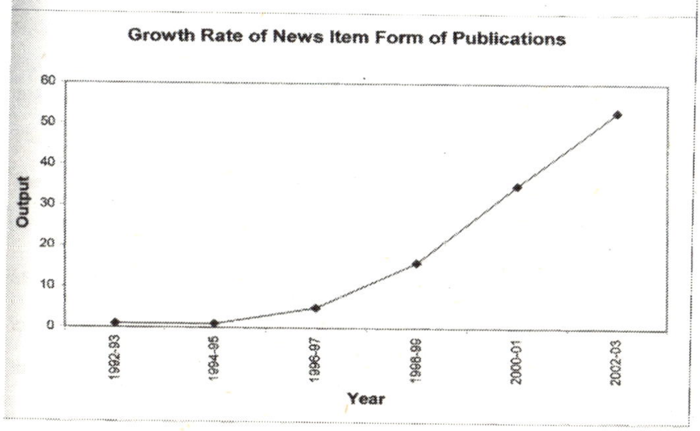

It could be seen clearly from the above discussion that the mean relative growth rate of news item form of Gender Studies in Informatics has shown an increasing trend and the mean doubling time for publication has shown a declining trend.

Table 13. Relative Growth Rate of Project and Online Discussion Form of Research Output in Gender Studies in Informatics

Year	Total Output	Cumu-lative		w2	R(a)	Mean (a) 1-2	Doubling Time	Mean pt (a) 1-2
1996-97	12	12	-	2.48	-	-	-	
1998-99	85	97	2.48	4.57	2.09	-	0.33	
2000-01	7	104	4.57	4.64	0.07	-	9.9	
2002-03	2	106	4.64	4.66	0.02	0.73	34.65	14.96

Source: Online Resources

Data presented in table 13 indicate the relative growth rate of project and online discussion form of research output in Gender Studies in Informatics. The relative growth rate has declined from 2.09 in 1998-99 to 0.02 in 2002-03. The whole period records a relative growth rate of 0.73.

The doubling time of publication of project and online discussion form of literature in Gender Studies in Informatics is worked out to 0.33 years in 1998-99 and it has risen to 34.65 years in 2002-03. The mean doubling time of publication is worked out to 14.96 years. The year 1998-99 records the highest level of project and online discussion forms of research output in Gender Studies in Informatics.

It could be seen clearly from the above discussion that the relative growth rate of project and discussion form of literature output has shown a declining trend. Contrastingly, the doubling time of publication has shown a massive level of increasing trend.

Chart – 8

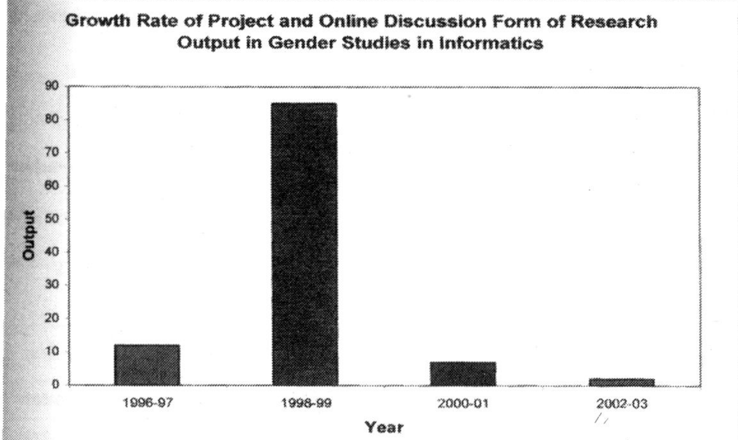

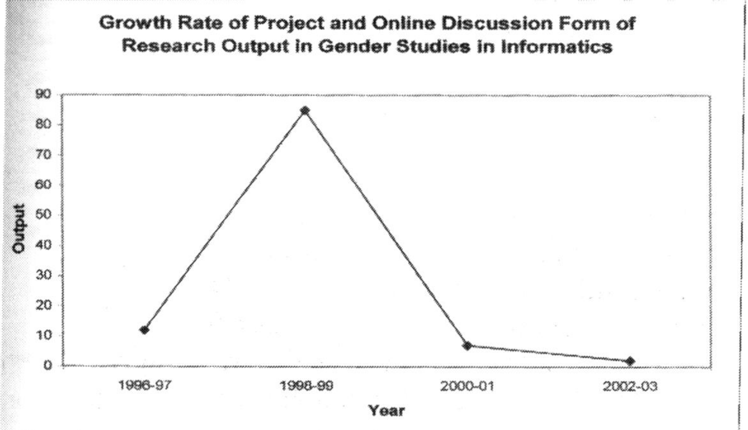

Data presented in table 14 indicate the journal article form of research output in Gender Studies in Informatics of the North American continent. It could be noted that the relative growth rate of North American continent has decreased from 0.407 in 1984-85 to 0.37 in 2002-03. However, the years 1988-89, 1992-93, 1994-95 and 1998-99 are out of trend. In general, the mean relative growth has shown an increasing trend during the study period as it has worked out to 0.57. The mean relative growth rate for the period 1984-85 and 1992-93 is worked out to 0.59 and it is 0.58 during the period 1994-95 and 2002-03.

Table 14. Relative Growth Rate of Europe Publications in Gender Studies in Informatics

Year	Total Output	Cumu-lative		w2	R(a)	Mean (a) 1-2	Doubling Time	Mean pt (a) 1-2
1986-87	2	2	-	0.23	-	-	-	
1988-89	2	2	0.23	1.05	0.82		0.85	
1990-91	54	7	1.05	4.34	3.29		0.21	
1992-93	2	79	4.34	4.37	0.03		23.1	
1994-95	14	93	4.37	4.53	0.16	1.075	4.33	7.12
1996-97	49	142	4.53	4.96	0.43		1.61	
1998-99	25	167	4.96	5.12	0.16		4.33	
2000-01	37	204	5.12	5.32	0.2		3.47	
2002-03	24	228	5.32	5.43	0.11	0.225	6.3	3.93
Total	228					0.65		5.53

Source: Online Resources

The doubling time of publication of literature of Gender Studies in Informatics of the North American continent has shown a marginal increase from 1.7 years in 1984-85 to 1.87 in 2002-03. However, the overall study period has shown a declining trend in doubling time of publication of literature on Gender Studies in Informatics. The mean doubling time for the period 1984-85 and 1992-93 is worked out to 1.46 years and it is 1.32 years for the period 1994-95 to 2002-03.

It could be seen clearly from the above discussion that at the overall level the relative growth rate has shown an increasing trend in the use of research output of the North

American continent literature, whereas the doubling time of publication has shown a declining trend in this connection.

A study of data in table 15 indicates the relative growth rate of Gender Studies in Informatics in American continent. It could be noted that the relative growth rate of the European continent literature has declined from 0.82 in 1988-89 to 0.11 in 2002-03. The year 1990-91 is out of trend due to the highest increasing trend in publication of literature. The mean relative growth rate for the period 1988-89 to 1994-95 is worked out to 1. 075 and it is 0.225 for the period 1996-97 to 2002-07. The mean relative growth rate for the whole period is worked out to 0.65.

Chart – 9

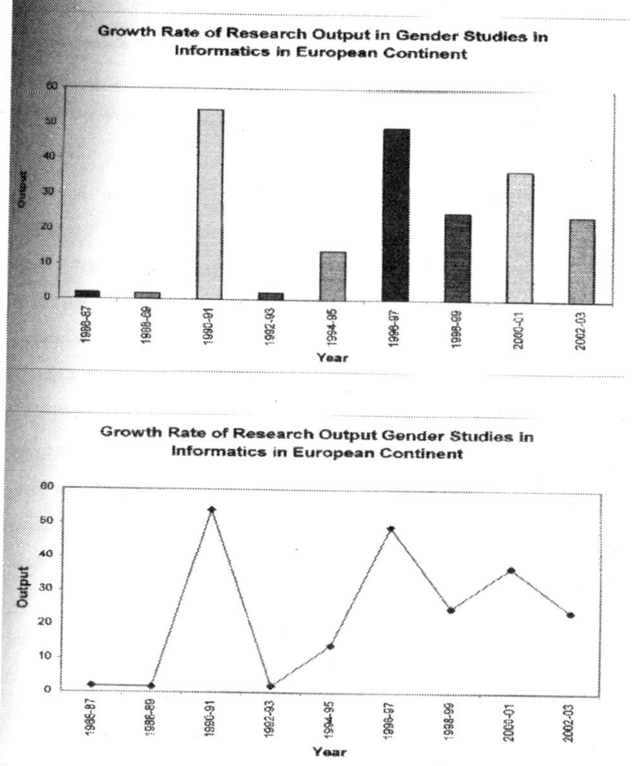

Table 15. Relative Growth Rate of Research Output in the North American Continent

Year	Total Output	Cumu- lative		w2	R(a)	Mean (a) 1-2	Doubling Time	Mean pt (a) 1-2
1982-83	2	2	-	0.693	-	-	-	
1984-85	1	3	0.693	1.1	0.407	-	1.7	
1986-87	1	4	1.1	1.39	0.29		2.39	
1988-89	9	13	1.39	2.56	1.17		0.59	
1990-91	7	20	2.56	3	0.44		1.58	
1992-93	19	39	3	3.66	0.66	0.59	1.05	1.46
1994-95	42	81	3.66	4.39	0.73		0.95	
1996-97	61	142	4.39	4.96	0.57		1.22	
1998-99	146	288	4.96	5.66	0.7		0.99	
2000-01	157	445	5.66	6.1	0.44		1.58	
2002-03	198	643	6.1	6.47	0.37	0.58	1.87	1.32
Total	643					0.57		1.39

Source: Online Resources

The doubling time of publication of European continent literature has increased from 0.85 years in 1988-89 to 6.3 years in 2002-03. The mean doubling time of publication of Gender Studies in Informatics of European continent is worked out to 7.12 years for the period 1988-89 -1994-95 and 3.93 years for the period 1996-97 to 2002-03. The whole study has a mean doubling time of publication which is worked out to 5.53 years.

It could be seen clearly from the above discussion that the relative growth rate of European continent has shown a declining trend with the exception of the year 1990-91. Contrastingly, the mean doubling time of publications has shown an increasing trend in this connection.

Table 16. Relative Growth Rate of Literature in Gender Studies in Informatics in the Australian Continent

Year	Total Output	Cumulative		w2	R(a)	Mean (a) 1-2	Doubling Time	Mean pt (a) 1-2
1994-95	3	3	-	1.1	-		-	
1996-97	9	12	1.1	2.48	1.38		0.5	
1998-99	3	15	2.48	2.71	0.23		3.01	
2000-01	7	22	2.71	3.09	0.38		1.82	
2002-03	2	24	3.09	3.18	0.09	0.52	7.7	3.26
Total	**24**							

Source: Online Resources

Data presented in table 16 indicate the relative growth rate of literature in Gender Studies in Informatics of the Australian continent. The relative growth rate has declined from 1.38 in 1996-97 to 0.04 in 2002-03. The mean relative growth rate for the whole period is worked out to 0.52. The doubling time of publications of literature in Gender Studies in Informatics has increased from 0.5 years in 1996-97 to 7.7 years in 2002. The mean doubling time of publication of the Australian continent literature is 3.26 years.

It could be seen clearly from the above discussion that the relative growth rate of the Australian continent literature has shown a declining trend whereas the doubling time of publication of literature has shown a increasing trend, indicating large time taken in doubling the number of research output in Gender Studies in Informatics.

Table 17 presents data on the relative growth rate of literature in Gender Studies in Informatics of the Asian continent. The relative growth rate of literature has declined from 2.397 in 1998-99 to 1.36 in 2002-03. There is a heavy shortfall in output in 2000-01. The whole study records the mean relative growth rate of 1.3.

Chart – 10

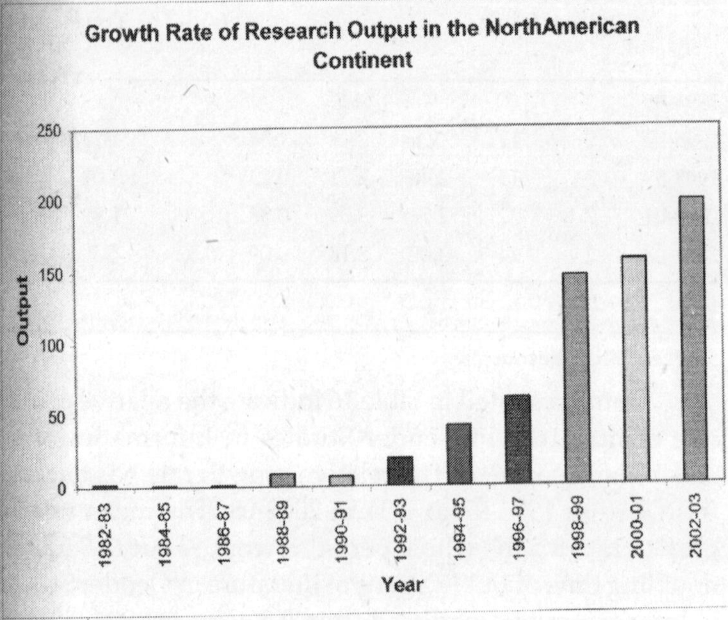
Growth Rate of Research Output in the NorthAmerican Continent
Output
250
200
150
100
50
0
1982-83
1984-85
1986-87
1988-89
1990-91
1992-93
1994-95
1996-97
1998-99
2000-01
2002-03
Year

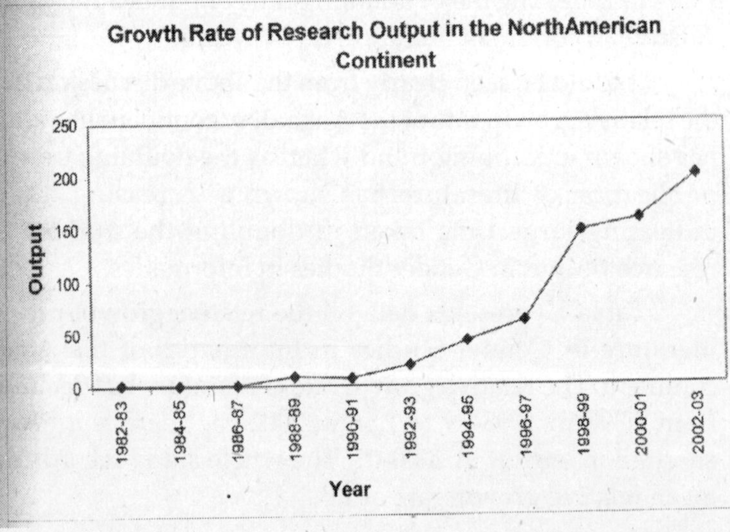
Growth Rate of Research Output in the NorthAmerican Continent
Output
250
200
150
100
50
0
1982-83
1984-85
1986-87
1988-89
1990-91
1992-93
1994-95
1996-97
1998-99
2000-01
2002-03
Year

Chart – 11

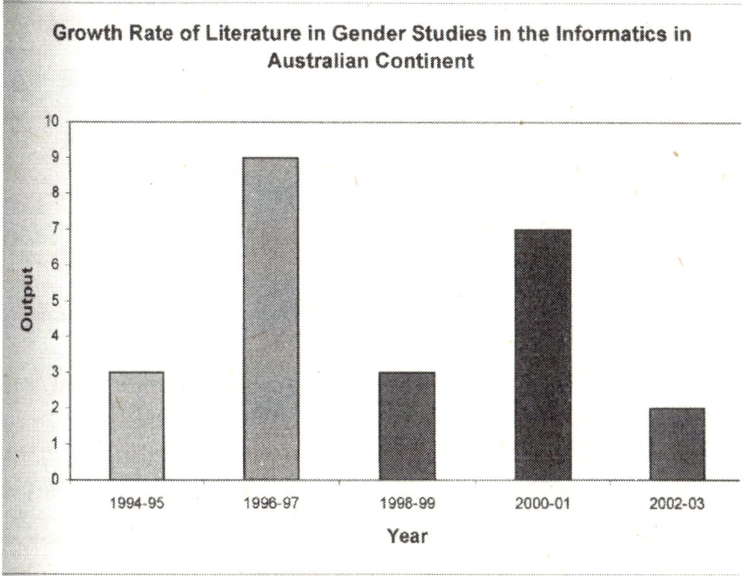
Growth Rate of Literature in Gender Studies in the Informatics in Australian Continent
Output
0
1
2
3
4
5
6
7
8
9
10
1994-95
1996-97
1998-99
2000-01
2002-03
Year

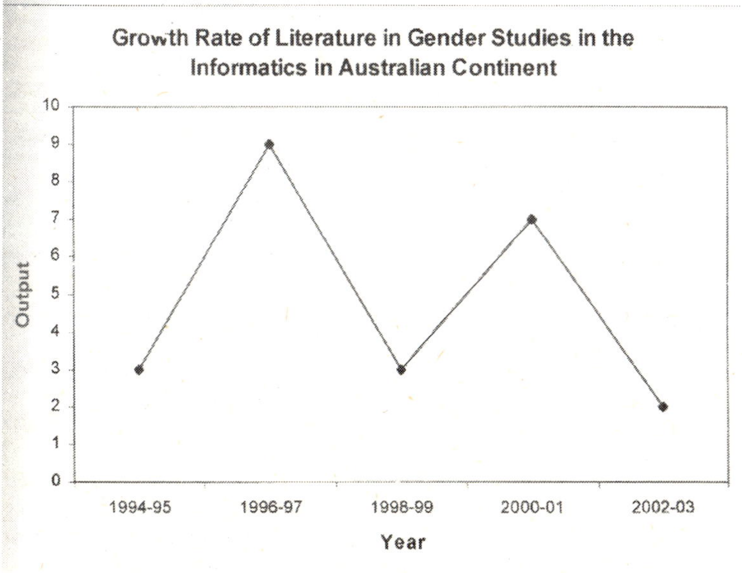
Growth Rate of Literature in Gender Studies in the Informatics in Australian Continent
Output
0
1
2
3
4
5
6
7
8
9
10
1994-95
1996-97
1998-99
2000-01
2002-03
Year

Table 17. Relative Growth Rate of Literature in Informatics in the Asian Continent

Year	Total Output	Cumulative		w2	R(a)	Mean (a) 1-2	Doubling Time	Mean pt (a) 1-2
1996-97	2	2	-	0.693	-		-	
1998-99	20	22	0.693	3.09	2.397		0.29	
2000-01	3	25	3.09	3.22	0.13		5.33	
2002-03	73	98	3.22	4.58	1.36	1.3	0.51	2.04
Total	98							

Source: Online Resources

The doubling time of publication of Asian continent literature has increased from 0.29 years in 1998-99 to 51 years in 2002-03. However, the year 2000-01 takes a lot of time to double the research output in gender studies in informatics. The whole study period records the mean doubling time of publication as 2.04 years.

It could be seen clearly from the above discussion that the relative growth rate of Asian countries literature has shown a declining trend whereas the doubling time of publication has shown an increasing trend.

Table 18. Relative Growth Rate of Research Output in the African Continent

Year	Total Output	Cumulative		w2	R(a)	Mean (a) 1-2	Doubling Time	Mean pt (a) 1-2
1992-93	8	8	-	2.08	-		-	
1994-95	1	9	2.08	2.2	0.12		5.78	
1996-97	13	22	2.2	3.09	0.89		0.78	
1998-99	19	41	3.09	3.71	0.62		1.12	
2000-01	8	49	3.71	3.89	0.18		3.85	
2002-03	3	52	3.89	3.95	0.06	0.37	11.55	4.62
Total	52							

Source: Online Resources

Chart – 12

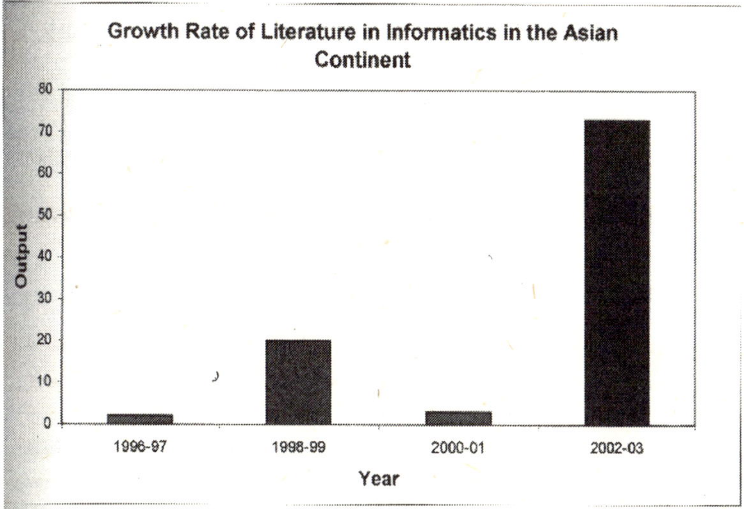

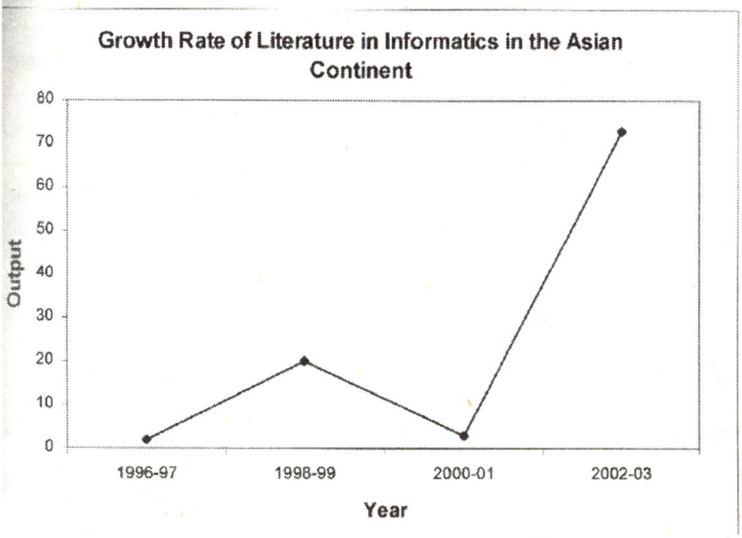

Data presented in table 18 indicate the relative growth rate of Gender Studies in Informatics of the African continent.

The relative growth rate of the African continent literature has decreased from 0.12 in 1994-95 to 0.06 in 2002-03. The years 1996-97 and 1998-99 have shown a deviation as they record more number of publications. The mean relative growth rate for the whole period is said to be 0.37.

The doubling time of research output in the African continent has increased from 5.78 year in 1994-95 to 11.55 years in 2002-03. The increase in doubling time is said to have a declining trend in publication of literature. The mean doubling time of whole period is said to be 4.62 years.

It could be seen clearly from the above discussion that the relative growth rate of the African continent literature has shown a declining trend. Contrastingly, the doubling time of publications has shown an increasing trend.

A study of data in table 19 indicates the country-wise index of performance of research output in Gender Studies in Informatics with reference to the African continent. It could be noted that totally 52 papers have been in the continent during 1982-83 and 2002-03. The annual average publication of research output in this continent is worked out to 0.174.

Among the countries in the African continent South Africa records the highest level of index value (718.39%) and at the global level its index value is worked out to 131.57. Nigeria takes the next position in its research output in Gender Studies in Informatics during the study period as its regional index value is 229.28. However at the global level, it has secured 42.10 as its index value.

More than 50 per cent of the continental index value has been observed in the countries, viz., Argentina (57.47%), Malawi (57.47%), Tanzania (57.47%), Tunisia (57.47%), Uganda (57.47%) and Zimbabwe (57.47%).

Chart – 13

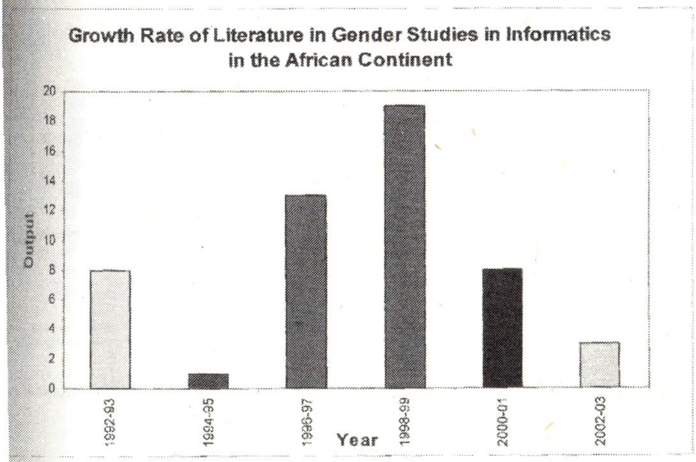

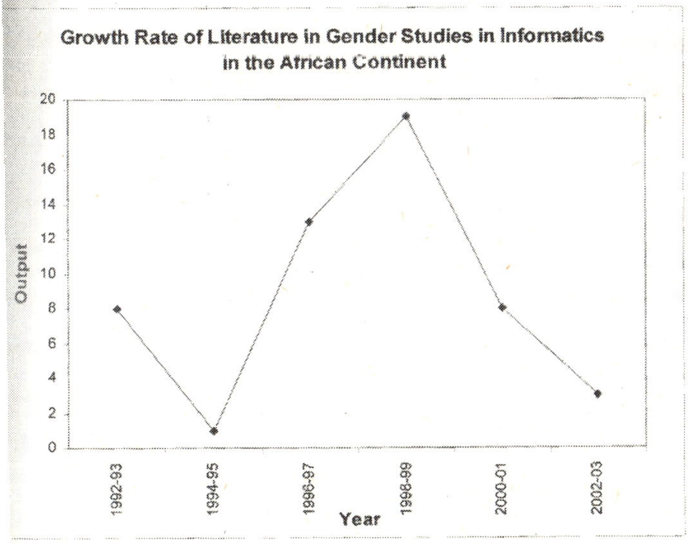

These countries at the global level have got an index value of 10.52 indicating that they are lagging behind at 89.48 per cent. In this study Burkina Faso, Ghana, Mali, Morocco, Sierra Leone and Zambia are put at the lowest level of contribution of research output in Gender Studies in Informatics.

Table 19. Country-wise Index of Research Output Performance in Gender Studies in Informatics in the African Continent

Country	Total Output	Annual Average	Relative Level Index Value at the Continent	Relative Index Value at the World Level
Burkina Faso	1	0.65	28.73	5.26
Ghana	1	0.05	2873	5.26
Malawi	2	0.10	57.47	10.52
Mali	1	0.05	28.73	5.26
Mauritius	1	0.05	28.73	5.26
Morocco	1	0.05	28.73	5.26
Nigeria	8	0.40	229.88	42.10
Sierra Leone	1	0.05	28.73	5.26
South Africa	25	1.25	718.39	131.57
Tanzania	2	0.10	57.47	10.52
Tunisia	2	0.10	57.47	10.52
Uganda	2	0.10	57.47	10.52
Zambia	1	0.05	28.73	5.26
Zimbabwe	2	0.10	57.47	10.52
Total	50	0.174	100	0.95=100.00
Average	3.57			
Annual Average	0.174			

Source: Online Resources

It could be seen clearly from the above discussion that the relative position of research output position is quite encouraging in South Africa as it stands above world average and it is considerable in the case of Nigeria. Some countries such as Burkina Faso, Ghana, Mali, Mauritius, Morocco, Sierra Leone and Zambia are at infancy state with respect to publications of research output in Gender Studies in

Chart – 14

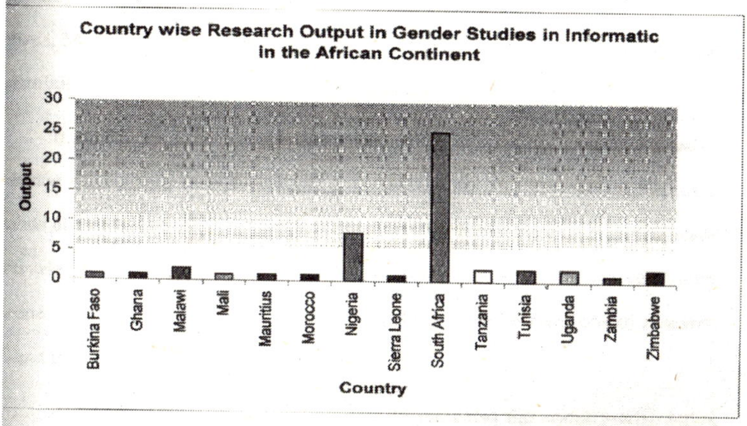

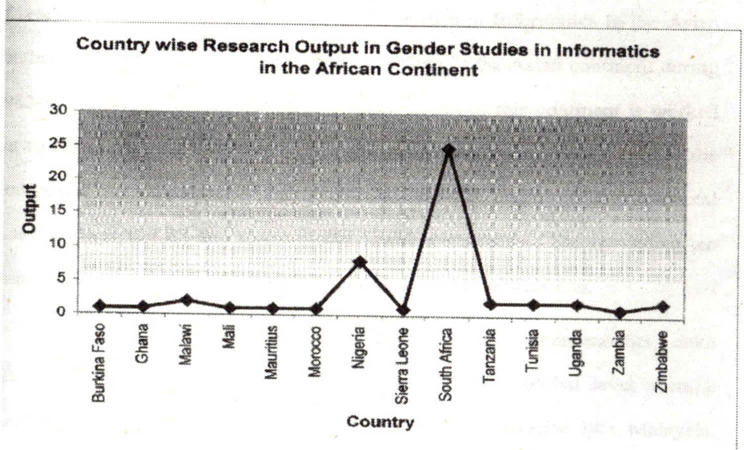

Informatics.

A keen observation of data in table 20 indicates the country-wise index of research output performance in Gender Studies in Informatics in the Asian continent. Totally 96 papers have been published in the Asian continent during 1982-83 and 2002-03. The average annual output of this continent is worked out to 0.44. Among the countries in the Asian continent, India occupies the first position with respect to publication of research output as its continental index value is 818.82 and at the global level, it is 378.95. The remaining ten countries have contributed 26.56 per cent of the total publications.

Countries such as Bangladesh, Indonesia, Israel, Japan and Sri Lanka have got only 10.52 index value with respect to their global level average number of publications per year. The rest of the countries like Malaysia, Philippines, Singapore, and Thailand have got an index value of 5.26 with respect to their relative position of the global level of annual average number of publication of research output in Gender Studies in Informatics.

Table 20. Country-wise Index of Research Output Performance in Gender Studies in Informatics in the Asian Continent

Country	Total Output	Annual Average	Relative Level Index Value at the Continent	Relative Index Value at the World Level
Bangladesh	2	0.10	22.72	10.52
India	72	3.6	818.82	378.95
Indonesia	2	0.10	22.72	10.52
Japan	2	0.10	22.72	10.52
Malaysia	1	0.05	11.36	5.26
Philippines	10	0.5	11.36	5.26
Singapore	1	0.05	11.36	5.26
South Korea	3	0.15	34.09	15.78
Sri Lanka	2	0.10	22.72	10.52
Thailand	1	0.05	11.36	5.26
Total	96		100	0.95=100.00
Average	9.6	0.44		

Source: Online Resources

It could be seen clearly from the above discussion that in the Asian continent, the research output contribution of

Indian scholars is noteworthy and the remaining ten countries have shown poor performance in their annual average number of publications in relation to global level.

Chart – 15

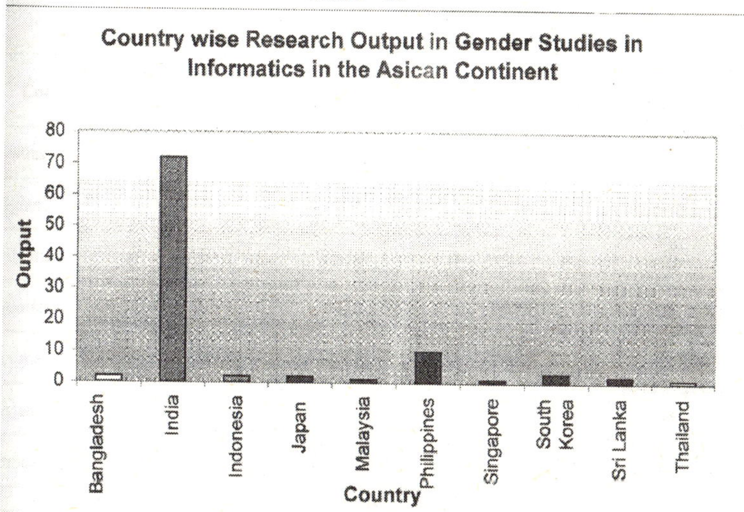

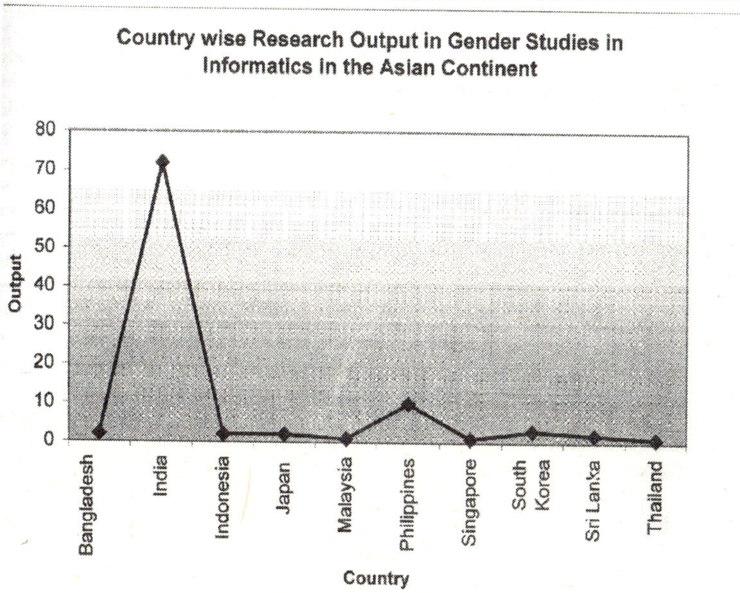

Table 21. Country-wise Index of Research Output Performance in Gender Studies in Informatics in the European Continent

Country	Total Output	Annual Average	Relative Level Index Value at the Continent	Relative Index Value at the World Level
Austria	3	0.15	23.80	15.78
England	1.58	7.9	1253.96	831.57
Bulgaria	2	0.10	15.87	10.52
Croatia	2	0.10	15.87	10.52
Denmark	3	0.15	23.80	15.78
Finland	3	0.15	23,80	15.78
France	6	0.30	47.62	31.57
Switzerland	3	0.15	23.80	15.78
Germany	8	0.4	63.48	42.1
Ireland	9	0.45	71.42	47.36
Italy	1	0.05	7.93	5.26
Jordan	1	0.05	7.93	5.26
Israel	2	0.10	22.72	10.52
Norway	3	0.15	23.80	15.78
Russia	3	0.15	23.80	15.78
Scotland	5	0.25	39.68	26.32
Sweden	2	0.10	15.87	10.52
The Netherlands	16	0.80	126.98	84.21
Total	230	0.63	100.00	0.95=100.00
Average	12.10			

Source: Online Resources

Table 21 presents data on the country-wise index of research output in Gender Studies in Informatics of the European continent. Totally 230 research papers have been published in Gender Studies in Informatics in the European continent during 1982-83 and 2002-03. The annual average publication of this continent is worked out to 0.63. Among the countries in the European continent, England records the highest position of research output in Gender Studies in Informatics as its continent level index value is 1253.96 and at the global level it is 831.57.

Chart – 16

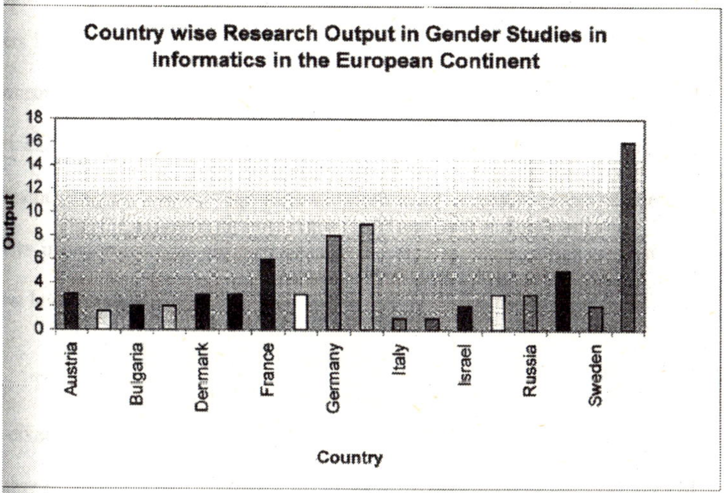

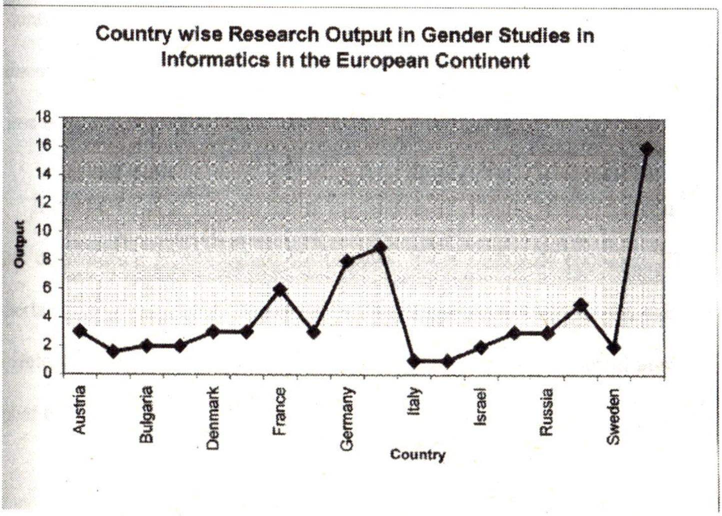

The research output of the Netherlands is above continental average as it is worked out to 126.98 and at the global level 84.21 in terms of annual average number Ireland and Germany have got an index value of above 50 per cent of the continental average among the eighteen countries chosen in the European continent, and the performance of eleven countries is very low since they have got less than 25 per cent of index value at the continental level.

It could be seen clearly from the above discussion that the research output contribution is the highest in England in the European continent. The Netherlands also records above continental level of research output. Germany, and Ireland have contributed more than 50 per cent of the continental annual number of research output in Gender Studies in Informatics.

Table 22. Country-wise Index of Research Output Performance in Gender Studies in Informatics in the Australian Continent

Country	Total Output	Annual Average	Relative Level Index Value at the Continent	Relative Index Value at the World Level
Australian	22	1.1	183.33	115.78
New Zealand	3	0.15	25.00	15.78
Total	24 12	0.6	100.00	0.95=100.00

Source: Online Resources

Data presented in table 22 indicate the country-wise index of research output contribution in the Australian continent. Only two countries in Australian continent have published research output. Between the countries in the continent, Australia occupies a predominant position in publication of research output in Gender Studies in Informatics as its continental level index value is 183.33 at the world level of 115.78. It is significant to note that New Zealand has got only 25 per cent of continental annual average number of research output and it is 15.78 per cent at the global level.

It could be seen clearly from the above discussion that New Zealand lags behind Australia in research contribution in Gender Studies in Informatics during the 20 years of the study period in terms of annual average number of publications.

Chart – 17

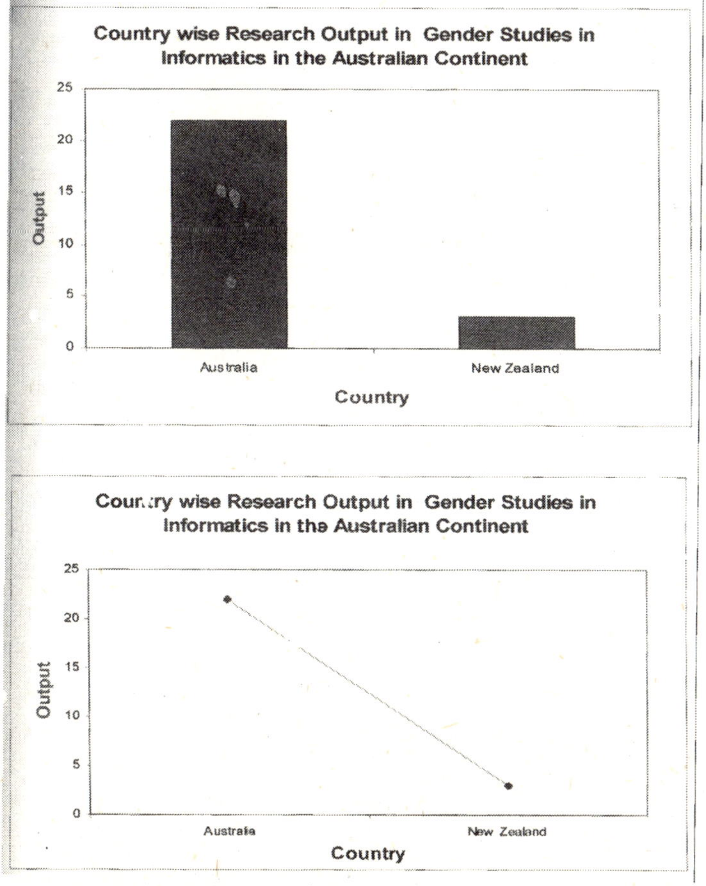

Table 23. Country-wise Index of Research Output Performance in Gender Studies in Informatics in the North American Continent

Country	Total Output	Annual Average	Relative Level Index Value at the Continent	Relative Index Value at the World Level
Canada	152	7.6	212.88	800.00
Central America	2	0.10	2.80	10.52
Guatemala	1	0.05	1.40	5.26
Mexico	2	0.10	2.80	10.52
USA	486	24.3	680.72	2557.88
Argentina	2	0.10	7.47	10.52
Total	645	3.67	100.00	0.95=100.00
Average	71.44			

Source: Online Resources

Table 23 depicts data on the country-wise index of research output performance in Gender Studies in Informatics with reference to the North American Continent. In this continent, nine countries have published 645 research output during 1982-83 and 2002-03. Among the countries in this continent, USA tops the list as its continental index value is worked out to 680.72 and at the global level it is 2557.88 in terms of annual average number of publication during the 20 years of the study period. Canada has come next in position as it has got its continental index value of212.88 and at the global index value of 800. The remaining countries have got less than 20 per cent of the annual average number of publications of the continent.

It could be seen clearly from the above discussion that countries such as Mexico, Guatemala, and Central America have got less number of index value at the continental value compared to world. The reason that North American continent shares more number of global publications of

Gender Studies in Informatics with USA as the topmost publisher in the world in Gender Studies in Informatics.

Chart - 18

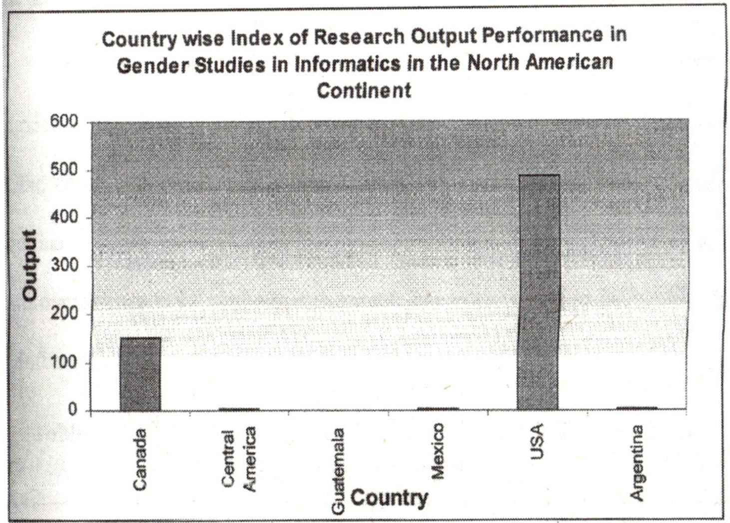

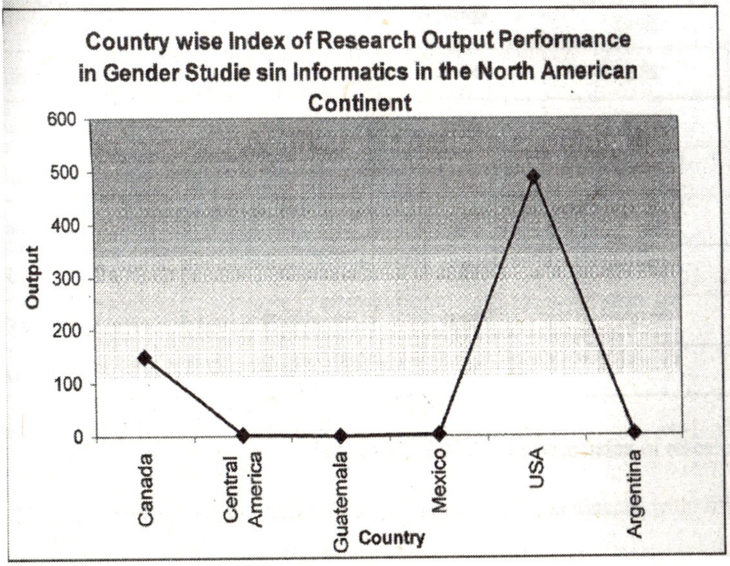

Table 24 Continent-wise Index of Research Output Performance in Gender Studies in Informatics

Continents	Total Output	Annual Average	Relative Index Value at the World Level
Africa	52	0.174	18.32
Asia	98	0.44	46.32
Australia	24	0.60	63.15
Europe	228	0.63	66.32
North America	643	3.57	375.78
Total 55 Countries	1045	0.95	100.00
Average	19		

Source: Online Resources

A study of data in table 24 indicates the continent-wise index of research output in Gender Studies in Informatics. Totally five continents with fifty five countries have published 1045 research output in Gender Studies in Informatics during 1982-83 and 2002-03. Among the continents in the world, North America takes more than 60 per cent the world output as it is evident from the index value of375.18. The remaining continents have got less number of index value, compared with global average index value of 100. The European continent comes next in position in contribution of research output in gender studies as its index value is 66.32 at the global level, Australian continent the third, Asian continent the fourth and Africa the last.

It could be seen clearly from the above discussion that North American continent occupies the top most position in the world is An contribution of research output in Gender Studies in Informatics particularly, the United States of America.

A study of data in table 25 indicates the journal source with index of research output in Gender Studies in

Informatics. Totally 349 papers have been published through 85 journal sources during 1982-83 and 2002-03. Among the 85 journals, 21 journals have published more than the total annual average level of publications during the period of analysis.

Chart – 19

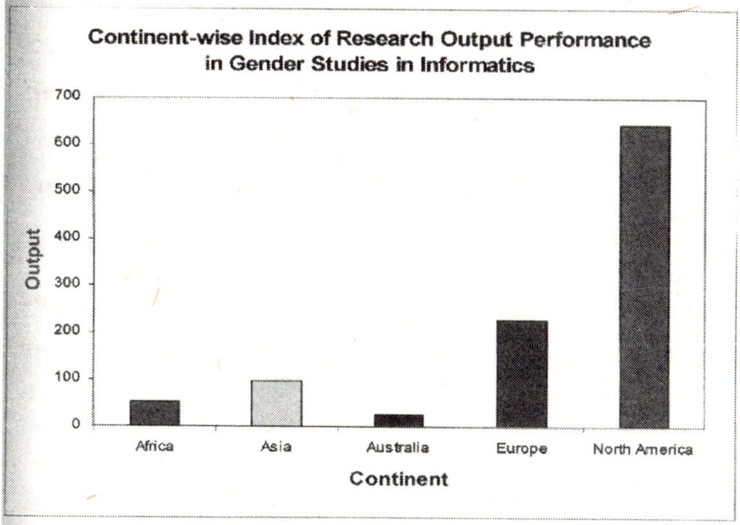

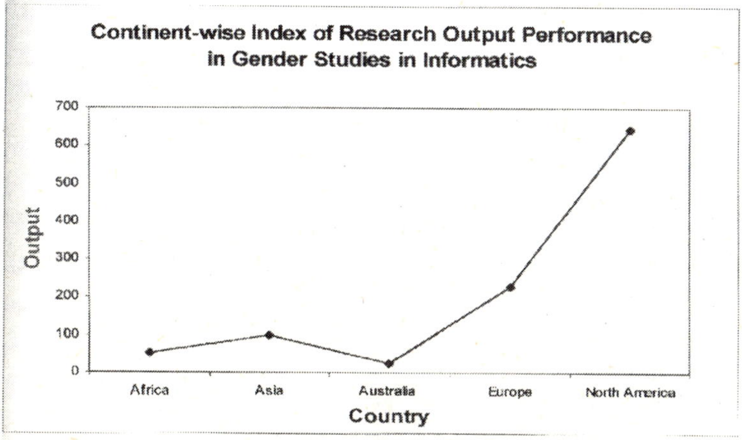

Among the journal sources the following journals have got an index value of above 500 viz., ACM SIGCSE bulletin, computing education and computer weekly. Some journals have got an index value in the range of 200- 500. They are communication of the ACM, Gender education, journal of educational computing.

Table 25. Journal Source of Research Output and their Performance to Overall Output

Journal	Total Output	Annual Average	Relative Journal Index	Relative Index Value to the Total Output
ACM SIGCSE Bulletin	36	1.8	900	900
Computing Canada	32	1.6	800	800
Computer Weekly	32	1.6	800	800
Communication of the ACM	18	0.90	450	450
Gender Education	16	0.80	400	400
Journal of Educational Computing	14	0.70	350	350
The Journal of New England Society	12	0.60	300	300
The CPSR New Letter	11	0.55	275	275
South African Computer Journal	11	0.55	275	275
Computer and Composition	10	0.50	250	250
Baltimore Magazine	10	0.50	250	250
Women and Technology	9	0.45	225	225
Journal of Women and Minorities in Science and Engineering	8	0.40	200	200
Gender Technology and Development	7	0.35	175	175
Women and the Internet	6	0.30	150	150
The Information Society	6	0.30	150	150
Women in Technology	5	0.25	125	125
Learning and Instruction	5	0.25	125	125

Higher Education in Europe	5	0.25	125	125
Women in Management Review	5	0.25	125	125
Emerald Information Technology and People	5	0.25	125	125
The Arachnet Electronic Journal of Virtual Culture	4	0.20	100	100
Mass High Tech	3	0.15	75	75
Info Word	3	0.15	75	75
ACM SIGCAS Computers and Society	3	0.15	75	75
Journal of Computer Meanted Communications	3	0.15	75	75
Journals Publish 2 Paper Each	22	0.10	50	50
Journal Publish one Paper Each	48	0.05	25	25
Total	349	0.20	100	100

Source: Online Resources

The journal of New England Society, The CPSR News Letter, South African Computer Journal, Computer and position Baltimore Magazine, Women and Technology and Journal of women and Minorities in Science and Engineering Nine Journals have got an index value between 100-200.

They are gender technology and development, Women and the Internet, The information Society, Women in Technology Learning and Instruction, Higher Education in Europe, Women in Management Review, Emerald Information Technology and People and Arachnet Electronic Journal of Virtual culture. In this study 11 journals have got 50 annual average index value and 48 journals have 25 annual average index value both at journal total and overall total of all sources.

It could be seen clearly from the above discussion that 72 journals have got below annual average level of publications as per the index value. The noted journals are ACM SIGCSE Bulletin, Computer Education, Computer

Weekly and Gender Education as they have more number of publications and also obtained the index score.

A study of data in table 26 indicates the performance of conference proceeding of publications in Gender Studies in Informatics during 1982-83 and 2002-03. Totally 479 conference proceedings have been published during the study period. It could be noted that out of the various conference proceeding forms of publications, ICWES-12 occupies the first position in relative index value of total conference proceeding form of publication as it is 525.25 in terms annual average index value. At the overall level its index value is 2600. WIT 2002 conference proceeding of publications takes the second place and its index value is 333.33 in the relative total of proceeding and IFIP 6th conference preceding the third.

The conference proceeding of IFIP occupies the fourth place, IFIP 7th the fifth. IFIP 5th the sixth, IEEE & 1ST As' 9th the seventh, IFIP 3rd the eighth, GASAT-8 the ninth and Technical Symposium Computer Science Education the tenth. These conference proceedings have above annual average limit of publications. The remaining conference proceedings have below annual average limit of publications.

It could be seen clearly from the above discussion that among the conference proceedings, ICWES-12, WIT 2002, IFIP 6th, IFIP 4th are noteworthy. In general, all the conference proceedings have above world annual average index value, indicating the predominant position of conference proceedings form of publication in Gender Studies in Informatics.

A keen observation of data in table 27 indicates the index of project form of research output in Gender Studies in Informatics. Totally 44 projects have been published by 18 projects during 1982-83 to 2002-03. Among the project form of publications, women in engineering advisory committee occupies the first position and its annual average index value is 666.67 in terms of total project form of publications and it is 400 with respect to overall output. , The women networking for education and training in technology takes the second position as its index value is 416.67 in the project level and 250 at the overall level. The projects GEM-Gender Evaluation Methodology and ISIS- International Manila each have 83.83 annual average index value. The remaining 14 projects cover 41.67 per cent of average of total project form of publications and it has 25 index value at the global level.

Table 26. Performance of Conference Proceeding Forms of Research Output in Gender Studies in Informatics

Conference Proceedings	Total Output	Annual Average	Relative Index Value of Conference	Relative Index Value to the Total Output
ICWES - 12	104	5.2	525.25	2600
WIT 2002	66	3.3	333.33	1650
IFIP 6th Conference	46	2.3	232.32	1150
IFIP 4th Conference	40	2.0	202.02	1000
IFIP 7th Conference	35	1.75	176.76	875
IFIP 5th Conference	32	1.6	161.62	800
IEEE-ISTAS-99	27	1.35	136.36	675
IFIP 3rd Conference	25	1.25	126.26	625
GASAT-8	23	1.15	116.16	575
Technical Symposium Computer Science Education	22	1.10	111.12	550
Women into Computing	17	0.85	85.85	425
The Women's Internet Conference	14	0.70	70.70	325
Special Interest Group on Computer Personal Research Annual	6	0.30	30.30	150
CSC & SIGCSE Technical Symposium	6	0.30	30.30	150

Science Conference	3	0.15	15.15	75.00
ACM Annual Computer Science Conference	3	0.15	15.15	75.00
ACM International Conference	2	0.10	10.10	50.00
Annual Joint Conference Integrating Technology into Computer	2	0.10	10.10	50.00
6 Conference Each 1 Output	6	0.05	5.05	25.00
Total	479	0.99	100	0.20=100
Average	19.95			

Source: Online Resources

It could be seen clearly from the above discussion that among the total project form of publications, Women Engineering Advisory Committee and Women Networking for Education and Training in Technology have above total of all sources of annual average number of publications. Most of the projects have best number of publications.

Table 27. Index of Project Form of Research Output in Gender Studies in Informatics

Project	Total Output	Annual Average	Relative Index Value of Projects	Relative Index Value to the Total Output
Women in Engineering Advisory Committee	16	0.80	666.67	400
Women Networking for Education and Training in Technology	10	0.50	416.67	250
GEM-Gender Evaluation Methodology	2	0.10	83.33	50.00
ISIS International Manila	2	0.10	83.33	50.00
Computing Research Association	1	0.05	41.67	25.00

European Social Fund	1	0.05	41.67	25.00
Gender Women and Development Working Group UNIFEM	1	0.05	41.67	25.00
ID2k-DFIDUK	1	0.05	41.67	25.00
MARS Millennium Project	1	0.05	41.67	25.00
SIG Research on Women and Education	1	0.05	41.67	25.00
SSHRC	1	0.05	41.67	25.00
The Canadian International Development Research Centre	1	0.05	41.67	25.00
The United States Agency for International Development	1	0.05	41.67	25.00
The University of British Columbia	1	0.05	41.67	25.00
The Womenadn Public Policy Programme	1	0.05	41.67	25.00
UNESCO	1	0.05	41.67	25.00
World Bank	1	0.05	41.67	25.00
Wisconsin Women's Studio	1	0.05	41.67	25.00
Total	44	0.12	100.00	0.20=100
Average	2.44			

Source: Online Resources

Data presented in table 28 indicates the index of news item form of publications in Gender Studies in Informatics. In this study 72 news form of publication have published 111 papers during 1982-83 to 2002-03. Among the news item form of output, Wired News and Business Wire have an annual average index value of 571.42 among the total news item of publications and it is 200 in the case of overall sources of publications.

News item like Canada New Wise and News Bytes New Network have an annual average index value of 357.15 among the total news item and it is 125 at the overall level of output. Internet New-Corn's annual average index value is

285.72 at the news item total level and it is 100 at the overall total level. Four sources have 75 index value of publications at the overall sources of publications. Three sources have 50 per cent of the index value of the total sources publishing Gender Studies in Informatics. It is interesting to note that 60 sources each by 25 index value of the total overall sources publish research output in Gender Studies in Informatics.

Table 28. Index of News item Form of Research Output in Gender Studies in Informatics

News Item	Total Output	Annual Average Output	Relative Index Value of News Item	Relative Index Value to the Total Output
Wired News	3	0.40	571.42	200
Business Wire	8	0.40	571.42	200
Canada New Wire	5	0.25	357.15	125
Newsbytes New Network	5	0.25	357.15	125
Internet News-Cum	4	0.20	285.72	100
Cisco Systems	3	0.15	214.28	75.00
2DNet	3	0.15	214.28	75.00
Silliconvalley-Com	3	0.15	214.28	75.00
Vonews-OM	3	0.15	214.28	75.00
CNW	2	0.10	142.85	50.00
BBC News	2	0.10	142.85	50.00
Women in Action	2	0.10	142.85	50.00
60 Items Publish Each One	60	0.05	71.42	25.00
Total	111	0.07	100.00	0.20=100
Average	1.54			

Source: Online Resources

It could be seen clearly from the above discussion that news item of Wired News and Business Wire are noteworthy in publishing Gender Studies in Informatics. In this study most of the news item are published by each source.

Table 29. Index Source-wise Research Output in Gender Studies in Informatics

Source	Total Output	Average Value	Index Value
Conference Proceedings	479	0.99	495
Journal Article	349	0.20	100
News item	111	0.07	35.00
Project Form	44	0.12	60.00
Online Discussion	62	0.05	25.00
Total	1045	0.20	0.20
Average Total Sources=261	4.00		

Source: Online Resources

A study of data in table 29 indicates the index of source with publication of research output in Gender Studies in Informatics. Among the sources conference proceeding forms of publication record 495 annual average index value of publication of research output in Gender Studies in Informatics and journal article records 100 as index value. News item form of publications have 35 index value of annual average number of publication among the sources of publishing literature on Gender Studies in Informatics, and it is 60 index value in the use of project form of publishing sources. Online form of publications has an annual average index value of 25.

It could be seen clearly from the above discussion that conference proceedings form of publications occupy the first position with respect to all sources of publishing literature in Gender Studies in Informatics, journal article source the second, project source the third, news item source the fourth and online discussion source the last.

A study of data in table 30 indicates the authorship pattern in Gender Studies in Informatics. It could be noted that the single author contributed paper was 2 in 1982-83 and it rose to 198 in 2002-03, indicating 45 per cent of annual growth rate during the period of analysis. The growth of single authored paper is not impressive from 1982-83 to 1994-95 and thereafter a rapid increase in multiplication of single authored paper has been observed.

Table 30. Authorship Pattern in Research Output in Gender Studies in Informatics

Year	Single	Double	Triple	Four	Five	Above 5	Total
1982-83	i (100)	-	-	-	-	-	2
1984-85	1 (100)	-	-	-	-	-	1
1986-87	3 (100)	-	-	-	-	-	3
1988-89	18 (60)	8 (26.67)	2 (6.67)	1 (3.33)		1 (3.33)	30
1990-91	49 (80.33)	7 (11.48)	5 (8.2)	-	-	-	61
1992-93	22 (75.86)	2 (6.9)	4 (13.79)	-	1 (3-45)	-	29
1994-95	46 (76.67)	5 (8.33)	3 (5)	4 (6.67)	2 (3.33)	-	60
1996-97	85 (63.43)	37 (27.61)	6 (4.48)	3 (2.24)	1 (7.46)	2 (1-49)	134
1998-99	164 (77)	38 (17.84)	4 (1.88)	29 (0.94)	4 (1-88)	1 (90.47)	134
2000-01	116 (54.72)	69 (32.55)	12 (5.66)	6 (2.83)	4 (1.89)	5 (2.36)	212
2002-03	198 (66)	46 (15.33)	39 (13)	13 (4.33)	-	4 (1.33)	300
Total	704 (67.37)	212 (20.29)	75 (7.18)	29 (2.78)	12 (1.15)	13 (1.24)	1045

Source: Online Resources

Figures in parentheses denote percentage

The number of double authored papers in Gender Studies in Informatics has 8 in 1988-89 and it rose to 46 in

2002-03, showing 4.67 per cent of annual growth rate during the period of analysis. The growth of double authored papers has not been reported till 1986-87 and thereafter they appeared, because the research activity in Gender Studies in Informatics has not received the attention of the scholar during 1982-83 and 1986-87.

The number of triple authored paper was 2 in 1988-89 and it rose to 39 in 2002-03 showing 231.25 per cent of annual average growth rate during the period of analysis. The triple authored papers have not been published in the journals and other forms of publications till 1986-87. The number of 4 authored paper was 1 in 1988-89 and it rose to 13 in 2002-03, indicating 150 per cent of annual growth rate during the study period.

The number of 5 authored paper was 1 in 1992-93 and it rose to 4 in 2000-01 and such type of authored paper was not reported in 2002-03. In this study, more than 5 authored paper was 2 in 1996-97 and it rose to 4 in 2002-03, showing 25 per cent of annual growth rate during the study period.

It could be seen clearly from the above discussion that more than two- thirds of the research papers in Gender Studies in Informatics are single authored papers. The double authored papers come next in order, triple authored paper the third, four authored paper the fourth, above 5 authored papers the fifth and five authored papers the last. It could be noted that when the number of authors increases, their proportion of contributed papers decreases and the vice versa.

Data presented in table 31 indicate the proportion of single vs multi- authored papers in gender studies. It could be noted that out of the total 10.45 papers published in this area, 67.37 per cent of them are single authored papers and the rest 32.63 per cent of them are multi-authored papers. The multi- authored papers have not appeared during 1982-

83 and 1986-87. It was in infancy in the growth of literature in Gender Studies in Informatics. During this period only a few papers appeared.

Table 31. Single Vs Multi-Authored Papers

Year	Single Authored Paper	Multi-authored Papers	Total
1982-83	2(100)	-	2
1984-85	1 (100)	-	1
1986-87	3 (100)	-	3
1988-89	18(60)	12(40)	30
1990-91	49 (80.33)	12 (19.67)	61
1992-93	22(75.86)	7 (24.14)	29
1994-95	46(76.67)	14 (23.33)	60
1996-97	85(63.43)	49 (36.57)	134
1998-99	164 (77)	49 (23)	213
2000-01	116 (54.72)	96 (45.28)	212
2002-03	198 (66)	102 (34)	300
Total	704 (67.37)	341	1045

Source: Online Resources

Figures in parentheses denote percentage

It could be seen clearly from the above discussion that single authored papers predominate the research output in Gender Studies in Informatics during the study period.

Table 32. Degree of Collaboration in Research Output in Gender Studies

Period	Single Authored paper	Multi-Authored Paper	Total	Collaboration
1982-91	73	24	97	0.25
1992-99	317	119	436	0.27
2000-03	314	198	512	0.38
Total	704	341	1045	0.33

Source: Online Resources

Figures in parentheses denote percentage

A study of data in table 32 indicates the degree of collaboration in research output in Gender Studies in Informatics. The degree of collaboration is 0.33 during the study period i.e., out of the total papers published only 33 per cent of them are published under joint venture.

During the period 1982-83 to 1990-91, the degree of collaboration was 0.25 and it rose to 0.27 during 1992-93 and 1998-99. Further, it rose to 0.38 in 2000-01 and 2002-03.

It could be seen clearly from the above discussion that the degree of collaboration in producing research output in Gender Studies in Informatics has shown an increasing trend during the study period since it is a new discipline.

Coword method is one of the tools of scientometrics articles from journals that are mostly used by scientists in a specific research field are excepted for a certain time period. The resulting databases describe the main development of a research field. Key words used to describe the content of an article are the basic building blocks of a research field. A cluster of keywords can be understood under a short description of a research theme. A research field is described as a structure of mutually connected research themes.

A study of data in table 33 indicates the continent-wise coword usage in Gender Studies in Informatics. It could be noted that 1045 source of publication of Gender Studies in Informatics have used 2831 cowords during the period 1982-83 to 2002-03. It could be noted that out of the total cowords 18.86 per cent of them deal with women in I.T. Education. Among the chosen continents North America shares 59.56 per cent of the cowords used in the literature in Gender Studies in Informatics, the European continent comes next in position (19.47%). This coword usage is the lowest in Australia. Of the total 2831 cowords used in the literature in gender studies 18.09 per cent of them discuss on women in I.T. employment. It is also found mainly in the literature published by North American scholars. There are 6.68 per cent of the cowords dealing with opportunities to women in I.T. sphere and a two third of them are published by North American scholars (72.48%).

Table 33. Continent-wise Coword Usage in Gender Studies in Informatics

Cowords	Africa	Asia	Europe	Australia	North America	Total
Women in IT. Education	28 (5.24)	60 (11.24)	104 (19.47)	24 (4.49)	318 (59.56)	534 (18.86)
Women in IT Employment	46 (8.98)	54 (10.55)	94 (4.24)	22 (4.24)	296 (57.82)	512 (18.09)
Opportunities to Women	4 (2.11)	10 (5.29)	32 (16.93)	6 (3.17)	137 (72.48)	189 (6.68)
Under Representation of Women in Employment, Education and Computing	26 (15.65)	60 (13.04)	76 (16.53)	28 (6.09)	270 (58.69)	460 (16.26)
Barriers in General	24 (6.03)	30 (7.54)	70 (17.58)	10 (2.51)	264 (66.34)	398 (14.06)
Gender Bias, Gender Gap, Gender Discrimination and Gender Equality	14 (3.36)	36 (8.65)	64 (15.38)	10 (2-40)	292 (70.29)	416 (14.69)
Male Domination	4 (4.59)	10 (11.49)	24 (27.58)	2 (2.29)	47 (54.03)	87 (3.07)
Absence of Women in Decision Making	4 (6.45)	6 (9.67)	12 (19.35)	4 (6.45)	36 (58.06)	62 (2.19)
Skill Shortage	4 (5.72)	2 (2.85)	22 (31.43)	2 (2.86)	40 (57.14)	70 (2.47)
Retention of women in computing	6 (13.33)	4 (8.88)	10 (22.22)	2 (4.44)	23 (51.14)	45 (1.58)

Ways to Attain Equality in Gender Access	8 (13.79)	6 (10.35)	10 (17.24)	4 (6.89)	30 (51.73)	58 (2.05)
Total	168 (5.94)	278 (9.82)	518 (18.29)	114 (4.03)	1753 (61.92)	2831 (100)

Source: Online Resources

Figures in parentheses denote percentage

Chart – 20

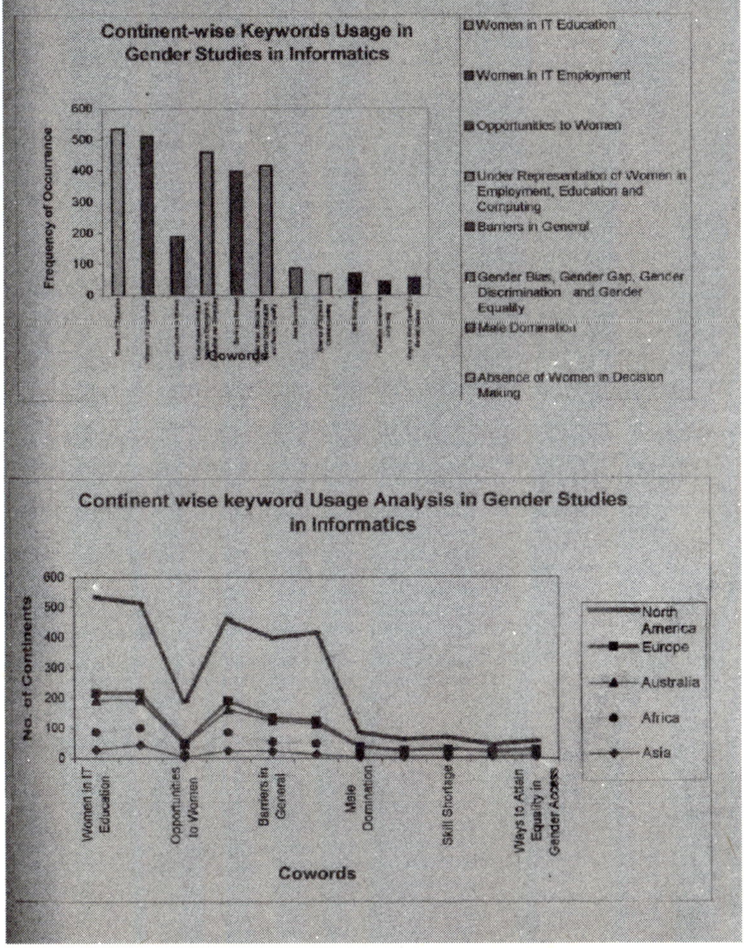

Of the total 2831 cowords used in the literature of Gender Studies in Informatics, 16.26 per cent of them relate to initiatives and strategies to promote women's participation in I. T. industry. African continents contribute to the lowest level of this coword (5.65%). Our of the total 2831 cowords applied in the literature of Gender Studies in Informatics 14.06 per cent of them are related to under representation of women in employment, education and computing. Australian continent is the lowest contributor of this coword. Among the total 2831 cowords used in the study 14.69 per cent of them deal with gender bias, gender gap, gender discrimination and gender equity. North

American scholars have contributed more than two-thirds of this coword usage (70.19%). Of the total 2831 cowords used in the study 3.07 per cent of them deal with male domination in I.T. industry. More than half of this type of cowords are contributed by North American scholars (54.03%).

There are2.19 per cent of the cowords which deal with the absence of women in decision making and 2.47 per cent of talk about skill shortage in IT business. Out of the total 2831 cowords used in the study, 1.58 per cent of them relate to retention of women in decision making and 2.05 per cent of them deal with ways to attain equity in gender access. It could be seen clearly from the above discussion that the cowords such as women in I.T. Education, women in I.T .employment, initiatives and strategies to promote women's participation in I.T. industry, under representation of women in employment, education and computing and gender bias, gender gap, gender discrimination and gender equity occupy a predominant position in Gender Studies in Informatics as they represent more than 10 per cent each one share in total cowords used in the study. The cowords like opportunities to women, male domination, absence of women in decision making, skill shortage, retention of women in decision making, and ways to attain equity in gender access share less in number with respect to overall cowords used in the study. Among the chosen continents North American continent shares 61.92 per cent of the cowords used in Gender Studies in Informatics. Europe comes next in position, Asia the third, Africa fourth in percent share of cowords used in Gender Studies in Informatics.

Table 34. Country-wise Coword Usage in Gender Studies Informatics in African Continent

Country	1992-93 to 1996-97	1997-98 to 2002-03	Total	Percentage to World Total
Women in I.T. Education				
Burkina Faso	1	-	1	0.187
Ghana	-	-	1	0.187
Malawi	1	1	2	0.374
Mali	1	-	1	0.187
Mauritius	-	1	1	0.187
Morocco	-	1	1	0.187
Nigeria	2	5	7	1.310
Sierra Leone	-	1	1	0.187
South Africa	2	3	5	0.936
Tanzania	-	2	2	0.374
Tunisia	-	2	2	0.374
Uganda	1	-	1	0.187
Zambia	-	1	1	0.187
Zimbabwe	-	-	-	-
Total	**8**	**18**	**26**	**4.866**
Women in IT Employment				
Ghana	1	-	1	0.195
Malawi	-	1	1	0.195
Mali	-	1	1	0.195
Mauritius	-	1	1	0.195
Morocco	1	-	1	0.195
Nigeria	2	4	6	1.172

Sierra Leone	1	-	1	0.195
South Africa	8	16	24	4.687
Tanzania	-	2	2	0.390
Tunisia	-	2	2	0.390
Uganda	2	-	2	0.390
Zambia	1	-	1	0.195
Zimbabwe	2	-	2	0.390
Total	**18**	**27**	**45**	**8.789**
Opportunities to Women				
Tanzania	2	2	4	2.11
Total	-	-	**4**	**2.11**
Initiatives and Strategies to Promote Women Participation				
Nigeria	2	9	11	5.820
South Africa	6	7	13	6.878
Total	**8**	**16**	**24**	**12.69**
Under Representation of Women in Employment, Education and Computing				
Nigeria	4	2	6	1.507
South Africa	4	12	16	4.020
Tunisia	-	1	1	0.251
Total	**8**	**15**	**23**	**5.778**
Gender Bias, Gender Gap, Gender Discrimination and Gender Equity				
Morocco	-	1	1	0.240
Nigeria	3	2	5	1.201
South Africa	2	5	7	1.683
Total	**5**	**8**	**13**	**3.12**
Male Domination				
South Africa	1	3	4	4.59
Total	**1**	**3**	**4**	**4.59**
Absence of Women in Decision Making				
Nigeria	2	-	2	3.23
South Africa	-	2	2	3.23
Total	**2**	**2**	**4**	**6.46**
Skill Shortage				
Nigeria	2	-	2	2.857

South Africa	-	2	2	2.857
Total	**2**	**2**	**4**	**5.714**
CountryRetention of Women in Decision Making				
Ghana	-	1	1	2.22
Nigeria	-	2	2	4.44
South Africa	1	1	2	4.44
Total	**1**	**4**	**5**	**11.1**
Ways to Attain Equity in Gender Access				
Mali	1	-	1	1.724
Nigeria	-	2	2	3.45
South Africa	2	2	4	6.89
Total	**3**	**4**	**7**	**12.066**

Source: Online Resources

Data presented in table 34 indicate the country-wise proportion of coword usage in Gender Studies in Informatics of the African continent. The African continent share 4.866 per cent of the women in I.T. Education at the global level. In the African continent fourteen countries have published research output in gender studies. Among the fifteen countries, fourteen countries have published coword for women in I.T .in their sources of publications. The countries that published coword include Argentina, Burkina Faso, Ghana, Malawi, Mali, Mauritus, Moroco, Nigeria, Sierra Leone, South African, Tanzania, Tunisia, Uganda, and Zambia. Zimbabwe has not published any coword for women in I.T. Education. Among these countries, Nigeria alone has more than 1 per cent of coword for women in I.T. Education in published and other global contribution is less than one per cent.

The coword women in IT employment is reported in thirteen countries scholars publications. Among them the publications of South Africa (4.68%) and Nigeria (1.17%) are noteworthy. The remaining countries record less than per cent of global share in use of coword number in I.T.

employment in their published literature in Gender Studies in Informatics. Totally, it shares 8.78 per cent of the global usage.

The coword opportunities to women are used by the scholar of Tanzania only and it shares 2.11 per cent of the global usage. The coword initiatives and strategies to promote women's participation shares 12.69 per cent of the global level usage in the literature of gender studies informatics. This coword is used in three African countries. Among them Nigeria (5.82%) and South Africa(6.87%) contributions are quite remarkable with respect to the global level of contribution.

The coword under representation of women in employment, education j and computing shares 5.78 per cent of the global level usage in the literature of Gender Studies in Informatics. This coword is found in the literature of four African countries and among them the contribution of South Africa (4.02%) is noteworthy at the global level of usage.

The coword of gender bias, gender gap, gender discrimination and gender equity shares 3.12 per cent of the usage at the global level source publishing Gender Studies in Informatics. The concept of male domination is represented only by South African scholars and it shares 4.59 per cent of the global level publication.

The concept usage of women in decision making shares 6.46 per cent of the global level usage. The concept is used in two countries, viz, Nigeria (3.23%) and South Africa (3.23%). The concept skill shortage shares 5.21 per cent of the global level usage and it is represented by the scholars of the two countries, viz., Nigeria (2.88%) and South Africa (2.86%). The coword retention of women in decision making shares 11.1 per cent of the global level usage in African continent. This coword is used by the scholars of Ghana, Nigeria and South Africa. The concept ways to attain equity to gender access share 12.06 per cent of the global usage and it is used by the scholars of Mali (1.72%), Nigeria (3.45%) and South Africa (6.89%).

It could be seen clearly from the above discussion that the cowords retention of women in decision making and ways to attain gender equity take more than 10 per cent of global share usage among the African continent scholars. Among the countries in the African continent, Nigeria and South Africa are the major contributors of cowords in Gender Studies in Informatics. The period 1992-93 and 1996-97 have witnessed relating less number of coword used in Gender Studies in Informatics. Many of the African countries have contributed less than 1 per cent of cowords used in Gender Studies in Informatics during the study period.

Data presented in table 35 indicate the country wise coword usage in Gender Studies in Informatics in the Asian continent. The coword women and I.T. Education shares 10.6 per cent of the total usage at the global level because of the growing demand for I.T. manpower in the industries across the world. It could be noted that eleven Asian countries have published research output in Gender Studies in Informatics during the period of analysis, viz., Bangladesh, India, Indonesia, Israel, Japan, Malaysia, Philippines, Singapore, South Korea, Sri Lanka and Thailand. Among the selected Asian countries, India shares the highest (7.30%) percentage contribution of coword women in I.T. Education. The remaining countries share less than one per cent of the world output each.

In the Asian continent, the coword women in I. T. employment shares 10.35 per cent of the world level usage coverage. Here also, India occupies the predominant position (7.23 %) in global share of coword women in I. T . Education and it is quite discouraging in the case of the remaining countries. In the Asian continent, the coword opportunities to women take 5.19 per cent of the global share as it is evident from a published literature. Only two countries to contribute to this type of coword, viz, India (3.70%) and Philippines (1.58%).

Table 35. Country-wise Coword Usage in Gender Studies in Informatics in the Asian Continent

Country	1992-93 to 1996-97	1997-98 to 2002-03	Total	Percentage to World Total
Women in I.T. Education				
Bangladesh	-	2	2	0.374
India	14	25	39	7.30
Indonesia	-	2	2	0.374
Japan	-	2	2	0.374
Malaysia	1	-	1	0.187
Philippines	3	2	5	0.936
Singapore	1	-	1	0.187
South Korea	2	1	3	0.561
Sri Lanka	1	1	2	0.374
Thailand		1	1	0.187
Total	**22**	**36**	**58**	**10.866**
Women in IT Employment				
Bangladesh	-	2	2	0.390
India	12	25	37	7.23
Indonesia	1	-	1	0.195
Japan	-	2	2	0.396
Malaysia	1	-	1	0.195
Philippines	1	3	4	0.781
Singapore	1	-	1	0.195
South Korea	2	-	2	0.390
Sri Lanka	-	2	2	0.390
Thailand	1	-	1	0.195
Total	**19**	**34**	**53**	**10.355**
Opportunities to Women				
India	2	5	7	3.70
Philippines	1	2	3	1.58

Total	3	7	10	5.19
Initiatives and Strategies to Promote Women Participation				
Bangladesh	-	2	2	0.434
India	23	30	53	11.521
Japan	2	-	2	0.434
South Korea	2	1	3	0.652
Total	**27**	**33**	**60**	**13.04**
Under Representation of Women in Employment, Education and Computing				
Bangladesh	2	-	2	0.502
India	7	10	17	4.272
Indonesia	2	-	2	0.502
Philippines	2	6	8	2.010
Thailand	-	1	1	0.251
Total	**13**	**17**	**30**	**7.537**
Gender Bias, Gender Gap, Gender Discrimination and Gender Equity				
Bangladesh	-	2	2	0.480
India	11	14	25	6.00
Indonesia	-	1	1	0.240
Philippines	2	4	6	0.240
Sri Lanka	1	-	1	8.65
Total	**14**	**21**	**35**	**15.61**
Male Domination				
Bangladesh	-	2	2	2.29
India	2	6	8	9.19
Total	**2**	**8**	**10**	**11.48**
Absence of Women in Decision Making				
Bangladesh	-	1	1	0.161
India	4	1	5	8.06
Total	**4**	**2**	**6**	**8.221**
Skill Shortage				
India	-	2	2	2.85
Total	**-**	**2**	**2**	**2.85**
Retention of Women in Decision Making				
Bangladesh	1	-	1	2.22

India	-	2	2	4.44
Japan	1	-	1	2.22
Total	**2**	**2**	**4**	**8.88**
Ways to Attain Equity in Gender Access				
India	2	2	4	6.89
Philippines	-	2	2	3.45
Total	**2**	**4**	**6**	**10.35**

Source: Online Resources

In this continent, the coword initiatives and strategies to promote women's participation in I.T. industry take 13.04 per cent of the global level coverage. This coword usage is prominent in four Asian Countries. Among them the highest usage is recorded in India (11.52%). It is significant to note that the coword under representation of women in employment, education and computing shares 7.54 per cent of the world level coverage. Five countries are the users of this work, of which it is quite remarkable in India (4.27%) and Philippines (2.01%) with respect to global level coverage of this coword in Gender Studies in Informatics.

In the Asian continent, the coword gender bias, gender gap, gender discrimination and gender equity take 15.61 per cent of the world coverage. Scholars of five countries have used this coword in their research papers and it is prominent among the Indian scholars (6%) with respect to world level coverage of this coword. The coword male domination shares 11.49 per cent of the global coverage and it is quoted by Indian scholars (9.19%) and Bangladesh scholars (2.29%). Similarly the coword absence of women in decision making is cited by the Indian scholars (8.06%) in the Asian continent. The coword skill shortage is represented only by Indian scholars (2.85%).

The coword for the retention of women in decision making shares 8.81 per cent of the world coverage. The coword was used by scholars of three countries in publishing their research output in Gender Studies in Informatics, viz., Bangladesh (2.22%), India (4.44%), and Japan (2.22%). In the Asian continent, the coword ways to attain equity in gender access shares 10.35 per cent of the usage at the global level. This concept draws attention among the scholars of two countries, viz., India and Philippines.

It could be seen clearly from the above discussion that among the chosen eleven Asian countries, Indian scholars are the prominent users of all cowords in publishing more reference output in Gender Studies in Informatics Philippines follows next in order. The coword male domination, Absence of women in decision making, and opportunities to women's ways attain equity in gender access received the attention of scholars of only two Asian countries. The cowords like women in I. T. Education and I. T. employment have received the attention of all scholars of Asian Countries in their published output on Gender Studies in Informatics.

Table 36 presents data on the country wise cowords share of European scholars publishing Gender Studies in Informatics during 1987-88, 1991-92 and 2002-03. The European continent scholars share 19.47 per cent of the coword women in I. T. Education with percent of the coword women in I.T. Education with respect to total usage at the global level. It could be noted that eighteen European countries publish research output in Gender Studies in Informatics, viz. Austria, Berlin, England, Bulgaria, Croatia, Denmark, Findland, France, Switzerland, Germany, Ireland, Italy, Jordan, Norway,Russia, Scotland, Sweden and The Netherlands. Among these countries, three countries have not contributed the coword for women in I. T. Education. Among the chosen countries England occupies the highest position in the European continent (11.98%) with respect to global share of women in I. T. Education coword usage followed by the with Netherlands (1.87%). The global share of the remaining countries is less than one per cent.

Table 36 Country-wise Coword Usage in Gender Studies in Informatics in European Continent

Country	1987-88 to 1991-92	1992-93to 1996-97	1997-98 to 2002-03	Total	Total Percentage to World
Women in I.T. Education					
Austria	1	-	-	1	0.187
England	22	18	24	64	11.985
Bulgaria	2	-	-	2	0.374
Croatia	1	-	1	2	0.374
Denmark	2	-	-	2	0.374
Finland	-	2	-	2	0.374
France	1	3	-	4	0.749
Switzerland	-	-	2	2	0.374
Germany	2	5	-	7	1.31
Ireland	-	1	-	1	0.187
Norway	-	1	-	1	0.187
Israel	-	2	-	2	0.374
Russia	2	-	-	2	0.374
Scotland	2	-	1	3	0.561
Sweden	-	-	1	1	0.187
The Netherlands	2	3	5	10	1.872
Total	**37**	**33**	**34**	**104**	**19.475**
Opportunities to Women					
Austria	-	2	-	2	1.058
England	-	3	6	9	4.761
Finland	-	-	2	2	1.058
France	2	-	3	5	2.645
Germany	2	3	-	5	2.645
Scotland	-	2	3	5	2.645
The Netherlands	-	-	4	4	2.11
Total	**4**	**10**	**18**	**32**	**16.931**
Women in IT Employment					
Austria	-	2	-	2	0.390

England	12	13	23	48	9.375
Bulgaria	-	-	1	1	0.195
Croatia	-	2	-	2	0.390
Denmark	2	-	-	2	0.390
Finland	-	-	5	5	0.976
France	-	-	2	2	0.390
Switzerland	3	-	2	5	0.976
Germany	2	1	4	7	1.367
Norway	-	-	2	2	0.390
Jordan	-	2	-	2	0.390
Israel	-	1	-	1	0.195
Russia	3	-	-	3	0.585
Scotland	-	-	1	1	0.195
The Netherlands	4	2	6	12	2.343
Total	**26**	**22**	**46**	**94**	**18.36**
Initiatives and Strategies to Promote Women Participation					
Austria	-	2	-	2	0.434
England	10	6	18	34	7.391
France	-	2	2	4	0.869
Switzerland	2	-	-	2	0.434
Germany	1	3	2	6	1.303
Ireland	4	-	2	6	1.304
Norway	-	-	3	3	0.652
Russia	-	-	2	2	0.434
Scotland	3	-	2	5	1.086
Sweden	-	2	-	2	0.434
The Netherlands	2	3	5	10	2.17
Total	**22**	**18**	**36**	**76**	**16.521**
Under Representation of Women in Employment, Education and Computing					
Austria		-	2	2	0.502
England	6	16	6	28	7.035
Bulgaria	-	2	-	2	0.502
Denmark	-	-	2	2	0.502
Finland	-	-	1	1	0.251

France	2	1	2	5	1.256
Germany	2	1	4	7	1.758
Ireland	2	2	4	8	2.010
Norway	-	2	-	2	0.502
Scotland	2	-	1	3	0.753
The Netherlands	2	3	5	10	2.512
Total	**16**	**27**	**27**	**70**	**17.58**
Gender Bias, Gender Gap, Gender Discrimination and Gender Equity					
Austria	-	-	2	2	0.450
England	6	10	12	28	6.730
Denmark	-	-	2	2	0.480
France	2	-	3	5	1.201
Germany	1	2	3	6	1.442
Ireland	2	2	3	7	1.682
Scotland	2	-	1	3	0.721
Israel	-	-	1	1	1.442
Sweden	-	-	1	1	0.240
The Netherlands	2	3	5	10	2.403
Total	**15**	**18**	**33**	**65.442**	**15.349**
Male Domination					
Austria	-	-	1	1	1.149
England	4	2	6	12	13.79
Germany	2	-	-	2	2.298
Ireland	-	2	3	5	5.147
The Netherlands	2	-	2	4	4.597
Total	**8**	**4**	**12**	**24**	**26.981**
Absence of Women in Decision Making					
Austria	-	-	1	1	1.62
England	-	-	2	2	3.24
Germany	1	-	2	3	4.84
Ireland	-	2	-	2	3.24
The Netherlands	2	-	2	4	6.45
Total	**3**	**2**	**7**	**12**	**19.39**

Skill Shortage					
Austria	-	-	1	1	1.42
England	3	4	3	10	14.28
France	-	2	2	4	5.71
Germany	2	-	3	5	7.14
Ireland	-	-	-	-	-
The Netherlands	-	2	-	2	2.857
Total	**5**	**8**	**9**	**22**	**31.407**
Retention of Women in Decision Making					
Austria	-	1	-	1	2.22
England	-	2	1	3	6.66
France	-	-	2	2	4.44
Germany	2	-	-	2	4.44
The Netherlands	2	-	-	2	4.44
Total	**4**	**3**	**3**	**10**	**22.22**
Ways to Attain Equity in Gender Access					
England	2	-	3	5	8.62
Germany	-	2		2	3.45
Sweden	-	2	1	3	5.17
Total	**2**	**4**	**4**	**10**	**17.24**

Source: Online Resources

The coword opportunities to women shares 16.93 per cent of the global coverage in the European continent. This coword usage is contributed by the scholars of seven countries, of which the contribution of the English scholars is quite remarkable (4.76%), at the global level. The European scholars share 18.36 per cent of the global usage of the coword women in I. T. employment in the published literature in Gender Studies in Informatics. This coword has got the attention of scholars of sixteen European countries. Of these the role of the English scholars (9.37%) and the Netherland scholars (2.34%) are quite remarkable.

It is significant to note that the coword initiatives and strategies to promote women participation shares 16.52 per cent of the global usage by the scholars publishing Gender Studies in Informatics. This coword usage is found among the scholars of twelve countries, of which the contribution of the English scholars (7.39%) and the Netherlands (2.17%) is noteworthy.

In the European continent the coword under representation of women in employment, education and computing shares 17.58 per cent of usage at the global level. The coword is contributed by the scholars of eleven countries. The contribution of scholars of England (7.03%), the Netherlands (2.51 %), Ireland (2.01%), Germany (1.76%) and France (1.26%) are noteworthy and the share of other countries is quite remarkable.

In the European continent the coword gender bias, gender gap, gender discrimination and gender equity share 15.34 per cent of the global coverage. Scholars of nine countries contribute to this type of coword in their published literature in Gender Studies in Informatics. The coword male domination shares 27.58 per cent of the usage at the global level source publishing Gender Studies in Informatics. This coword is contributed by the scholars of five countries, of which England shares (13.79%) the highest level of percentage coverage at the global level.

The coword absence of women in decision making takes 19.35 per cent of the coverage at the global level with respect to source publishing Gender Studies in Informatics. This coword is contributed by the scholars of five European countries.

In the European continent, the coword skill shortage takes the 31.43 per cent of the global coverage with respect to sources publication of Gender Studies in Informatics and it is contributed by the scholars of five countries. The coword retention of women in decision making shares 22.22 per cent of the world level coverage in the literature and it is also published by the scholars of five countries. In this continent the coword ways to attain gender equity shares 17.24 per cent of the global coverage and it is contributed by the scholars of three countries.

It could be seen clearly from the above discussion that all the cowords are not covered by all the eighteen European countries. Among the European countries, the scholars of England occupy the first position in their coverage of all cowords in their publication research output in gender studies informatics, followed by the Netherlands. The coword like absence of women in decision making, reference to women in decision making, ways to attain gender equity and male domination receive the attention of scholars of up to five Asia countries.

Table 37 presents data on the country wise cowords usage in Gender Studies in Informatics of the North American continent. The North American scholars share 59.93 per cent of the world women in I.T. Education usage at the global level participation of Gender Studies in Informatics. Nine North American scholars have published their research output in Gender Studies in Informatics, viz., Canada, Central America, Guatemala, Mexico, USA. Among these countries the scholars of USA top the list (48.87%) followed by Canada (9.74%) in their usage of coword women in I.T. Education. The share of the remaining countries is quite discouraging as it is less than one per cent.

In the North American continent the coword of women in I.T. employment shares 58 per cent of the usage at the global level literature. Here also the contribution of scholars of Canada (23.8%) and USA (32.32%) is quite remarkable. The coword opportunities to women take 72.48 per cent of coverage at the global level. The six scholars of the North American Continent also used this coword and it is mainly used by the scholars of USA (41.78%) and Canada (30.16%).

Table 37. Country-wise Coword Usage in Gender Studies in Informatics in North American Continent

Country	1982-83 to 1986-87	1987-88 to 1991-92	1992-93 to 1996-97	1997-98 to 2002-03	Total Percentage to World	Total
Women in I.T. Education						
Canada	1	10	10	31	52	9.74
Central America	-	-	-	2	2	0.374
Guatemala	-	-	1	-	1	0.187
Mexico	-	-	-	2	2	0.374
USA	3	33	38	187	261	48.87
Argentina	-	-	-	2	2	0.374
Total	**4**	**43**	**49**	**224**	**320**	**59.93**
Women in IT Employment						
Canada	2	6	18	96	122	23.83
Central America	-	1	1	2	4	0.781
Guatemala	-	-	1	1	2	0.390
Mexico	-	2	-	2	4	0.781
USA	2	13	36	113	164	32.32
Argentina	-	-	1	-	1	0.195
Total	**4**	**22**	**57**	**214**	**297**	**58.00**
Opportunities to Women						
Canada	-	8	10	39	57	30.158
Central America	-	-	1	-	1	0.529
USA	2	12	15	50	79	41.78
Total	**2**	**20**	**26**	**89**	**137**	**72.48**
Initiatives and Strategies to Promote Women Participation						
Canada	-	8	12	86	106	23.04
Central America	-	-	1	2	3	0.652
Mexico	-		2	2	4	0.869
USA	2	16	43	96	157	34.12
Argentina	-	-	-	2	2	0.434
Total	**2**	**24**	**58**	**188**	**272**	**59.12**

Under Representation of Women in Employment, Education and Computing						
Canada	2	6	18	53	79	19.85
Central America	-	-	-	1	1	0.251
Guatemala	-	1	-	1	2	0.502
Mexico	-	-	1	-	1	0.251
USA	8	45	41	87	181	45.47
Argentina	-	-	-	1	1	0.251
Total	**10**	**52**	**60**	**143**	**265**	**66.58**
Gender Bias, Gender Gap, Gender Discrimination and Gender Equity						
Canada	2	16	18	36	72	17.30
Central America	-	-	-	2	2	0.480
Mexico	-	-	-	1	1	0.240
USA	4	15	57	140	216	51.92
Argentina	-	-	1	-	1	0.240
Total	**-**	**-**	**1**	**-**	**1**	**0.240**
Average	**6**	**31**	**77**	**179**	**293**	**70.43**
Male Domination						
Canada	-	-	12	9	21	24.14
Central America	-	-	-	2	2	2.29
Mexico	-	2	-	-	2	2.29
USA	4	6	5	7	22	25.28
Total	**4**	**8**	**17**	**18**	**47**	**54.00**
Absence of Women in Decision Making						
Canada	-	2	3	9	14	22.58
Central America	-	1	-	1	2	3.23
Guatemala	-	-	1	-	1	1.62
USA	-	4	9	6	19	30.66
Total	**-**	**7**	**13**	**16**	**36**	**58.09**
Skill Shortage						
Canada	2	3	3	5	13	18.57
Central America	-	-	1	-	1	1.43
Guatemala	-	-	2	1	3	4.28
USA	2	4	8	9	23	34.28
Total	**4**	**7**	**14**	**15**	**40**	**58.56**

Retention of Women in Decision Making						
Canada	-	2	2	2	6	13.33
Central America %	-	-	1	-	1	2.22
USA	2	2	3	7	14	35.54
Argentina	-	-	1	-	1	2.22
Total	**2**	**4**	**7**	**19**	**22**	**53.31**
Ways to Attain Equity in Gender Access						
Canada	-	2	4	3	9	15.52
Central America	-	-	-	1	1	1.72
USA	2	2	3	13	20	34.48
Argentina	-	-	-	1	1	1.724
Total	**2**	**4**	**7**	**18**	**31**	**53.44**

Source: Online Resources

In the North American continent the coword initiatives and strategies to promote women participation shares 59.12 per cent of the global usage coverage. This coword is used by the scholars of five countries, of which the contribution of scholars of Canada (23.04%) and the USA (34.12%) of quite significant. The scholars of the North American continent share 66.58 per cent of the coword under representation of home in employment, education and computing at the global level in Gender Studies in Informatics. This coword is contributed by the scholars of seven countries of the North American continent with the major contribution by the scholars of USA (45.47%) and Canada (19.85%).

In the North American continent the scholars of informatics science share 66.58 per cent of the global coverage of the coword for gender bias, gender gap, gender discrimination and gender equity in their published research output. This coword is used by the scholars of six countries, of which USA (45.47%) and Canada (19.85%) are of noteworthy. The coword male domination shares 54 per cent of the global coverage. The scholars of six countries have used this coword in their papers. Here also Canadian and

Americans are the prominent contributors.

In the North American continent the scholars share 58.09 per cent of the global usage of the coword for absence of women in decision making. The scholars of six countries have used this concept, notably the USA and Canada. The coword skill shortage takes the 58.56 per cent of the global level usage in the literature publishing Gender Studies in Informatics. The scholars of four countries in the North American continent have used this concept. The coword retention of women in decision making takes 51.09 per cent of the usage in the literature publishing Gender Studies in Informatics at the global level, contributed by scholars of five countries. The scholars of the North American continent share 51.72 per cent of the coverage of the coword ways to attain equity in gender access. The scholars of five countries have used this coword in their publications on Gender Studies in Informatics.

It could be seen clearly from the above discussion that the scholars of the North American continent share more than half of the all cowords usage in literature publishing Gender Studies in Informatics. Among the North American continent countries, the scholars of the USA top the list, followed by Canada in using more proportion of all cowords in their published literature in Gender Studies in Informatics. The coword like women in I. T. Education and employment has drawn the attention of scholars' of all chosen countries of the North American continent. Usually the scholars coword usage level is quite discouraging in the contrasting Central America, Eugene, Green Ville, Guatemala, Mexico, Virginia, and West Field, since they have very less number of publications to their credit and ultimately they have less coword usage at the global share.

Data presented in table 38 indicate the country-wise coword usage in Gender Studies in Informatics of the scholars of the Australian continent. Only scholars of the two countries viz., Australia and Newzealand have contributed cowords in Gender Studies in Informatics. The scholars started publications only from 1992-93. Hence the period of analysis is related to 1992-93 to 2002-03. The Australian continent scholars share 4.49 per cent of the global usage of coword women in I. T. Education and also women in I. T. employment. In both cowords, the scholars of Australia predominates New Zealand in their percent of global coverage of their two cowords.

The coword opportunity to women shares 3.17 per cent of the global coverage in the Australian continent and it is 6.08 per cent in the case of coword initiatives and strategies to promote women participation. Here also the scholars of Australia are predominant over New Zealand in their global share of contribution.

The Australian continent scholars share 2.51 per cent of the usage of the coword under representation of women in employment, education and computing at the global level and it is 2.40 per cent in the case of coword gender bias, gender gap, gender discrimination and gender equity.

In the Australian continent the coword male domination shares 2.29 per cent of the usage at the global level and it is 6.45 per cent in the case of co word absence of women in decision making. The scholars of Australian continent share 2.86 per cent of the usage of the coword skill shortage at the global level in their publications and it is 4.44 per cent in the case of coword retention of women in decision making. In the Australian continent coword ways to attain equity in gender access takes 6.90 per cent of the usage at the global level.

It could be seen clearly from the above discussion that only scholars of the two Australian continent countries contributed cowords in Gender Studies in Informatics. The New Zealand scholars have not used the coword like skill shortage and male domination. The Australian scholars share

Table 38. Country-wise Coward Usage in Gender Studies in Informatics in Australian Continent

Country	Women in IT Education				Women in IT Employment				Opportunities to Women				Initiatives and Strategies to Promote Women Participation			
	1992-93 and 1996-97	1997-98 and 2002-03	Total	%age to World Total	1992-93 and 1996-97	1997-98 and 2002-03	Total	%age to World Total	1992-93 and 1996-97	1997-98 and 2002-03	Total	%age to World Total	1992-93 and 1996-97	1997-98 and 2002-03	Total	%age to World Total
Australian	10	12	22	4.11	8	13	21	4.10	1	4	5	2.65	5	13	18	3.91
New Zealand	–	2	2	0.375	1	2	3	0.195	–	1	1	0.529	–	10	10	2.17
Total	10	14	24	4.49	9	15	22	4.29	1	5	6	3.17	5	13	28	6.08

Country	Under Representation of Women in Employment, Education and Computing				Gender Bias, Gender Gap, Gender Discrimination and Equity				Male Domination				Absence of Women in Decision Making			
	1992-93 and 1996-97	1997-98 and 2002-03	Total	%age to World Total	1992-93 and 1996-97	1997-98 and 2002-03	Total	%age to World Total	1992-93 and 1996-97	1997-98 and 2002-03	Total	%age to World Total	1992-93 and 1996-97	1997-98 and 2002-03	Total	%age to World Total
Australian	3	4	7	1.76	2	5	7	1.68	–	2	2	2.29	1	2	3	4.53
New Zealand	1	2	3	0.753	1	2	3	0.72	–	–	–	–	–	1	1	1.62
Total	4	6	10	2.51	3	7	10	2.40	–	2	2	2.29	1	3	4	6.45

Country	Skill Shortage				Retention of Women in Decision Making				Ways to Attain Equity in Gender Access							
	1992-93 and 1996-97	1997-98 and 2002-03	Total	%age to World Total	1992-93 and 1996-97	1997-98 and 2002-03	Total	%age to World Total	1992-93 and 1996-97	1997-98 and 2002-03	Total	%age to World Total				
Australian	–	2	2	2.86	–	1	1	2.22	2	–	2	3.45				
New Zealand	–	–	–	–	–	1	1	2.22	–	2	2	3.45				
Total	–	2	2	2.86	–	2	2	4.44	2	2	4	6.90				

less proportion of all cowords usage at the global level in their published literature in Gender Studies in Informatics, since their number of publications is limited to 24 only.

Table 39. Duration-wise Coword Usage in Gender Studies in Informatics

Cowords	1982-83 to 1986-87	1987-88 to 1991-92	1992-93 to 1996-97	1997-98 to 2002-03	Total
Women in IT. Education	4 (0.74)	80 (14.98)	124 (23.22)	326 (61.06)	534 (18.86)
Women in IT Employment	4 (0.78)	48 (9.37)	126 (24.60)	334 (65.25)	512 (18.09)
Opportunities to Women	2 (1.06)	24 (12.69)	42 (22.22)	121 (64.03)	189 (6.68)
Under Representation of Wom in Employment, Education and Computing	2 (0.44)	46 (10.00)	116 (25.22)	296 (64.34)	460 (16.26)
Barriers in General	10 (2.51)	68 (17.08)	112 (28.14)	208 (52.27)	398 (14.06)
Gender Bias, Gender Gap, Gender Discrimination and Gender Equality	6 (1-44)	46 (11.05)	116 (27.88)	248 (59.63)	416 (14.69)
Male Domination	4 (4.59)	16 (18.39)	24 (27.58)	43 (49.44)	87 (3.07)
Absence of Women in Decision Making	-	10 (16.13)	22 (35.48)	30 (48.38)	62 (2.19)
Skill Shortage	4 (5.71)	12 (17.14)	24 (34.28)	30 (42.87)	70 (2.47)
Retention of women in computing	2 (4.44)	8 (17.78)	13 (28.88)	22 (48.9)	45 (1.58)

Ways to Attain Equality in Gender Access	2 (3.45)	6 (10.35)	18 (31.03)	32 (55.17)	58 (2.05)
Total	**40 (1.42)**	**364 (12.86)**	**737 (26.03)**	**1690 (59.69)**	**2831**

Source: Online Resources

Figures in parentheses denote percentage

Data presented in table 39 indicate the duration-wise coword used in Gender Studies in Informatics. It could be noted that there are 40 key word used during 1982-83 to 1986-87 in the literature of Gender Studies in Informatics, constituting 1.42 per cent of the total words used during the study period. The key word like women in I. T .Education, women in I.T employment and initiatives and strategies to promote women's participation share very less proportion during the period 1982-83 to 1986-87.

There are 364 cowords used in the literature of Gender Studies in Informatics during 1987-88 to 1991-92 constituting 12.86 per cent of total coword used in the study period. This period has witnessed an increasing trend with respect to each coword usage. It could be observed that during the period 1992-93 to 1996-97, 737 cowords have been used in Gender Studies in Informatics, constituting 26.03 per cent of the overall cowords used in the study period. More than half of the cowords usage in Gender Studies in Informatics (59.69%) has been used between 1997-98 and 2002-03.

It could be seen clearly from the above discussion that the highest number of cowords usage is found during the period 1997-98 to 2002-03, due to recording of the highest number of publications in Gender Studies in Informatics. The period 1992-93 to 1996-97 records second in order of cowords share with respect to the total number of cowords used in the literature of Gender Studies in Informatics the period 1987-88 to 1991-92 the third and "1982-83 to 1986-87 the last. The period 1982-83 to 1986-87 is said to be at the infancy stage for the shown, literature in Gender Studies in Informatics. Hence this period has less number of publications and key words usage and thereafter it has grown rapidly particularly during 1997-98 to 2002-03.

Table 40. Source-wise Coword Usage in Gender Studies in Informatics

Cowords	Conference Proceeding	Journal Article	News Item	Project Report	Online Discussion	Total
Women in IT. Education	228 (42.69)	178 (33.34)	92 (17.23)	4 (0.75)	32 (5.99)	534 (18.86)
Women in IT Employment	224 (43.75)	204 (39.84)	66 (12.89)	8 (1.56)	10 (1.96)	512 (18.09)
Opportunities to Women	75 (39.68)	82 (43.38)	22 (11.64)	6 (3.17)	4 (2.13)	189 (6.68)
Under Representation of Women in Employment Education and Computing	96 (20.87)	192 (41.74)	70 (15.21)	50 (10.86)	52 (11.30)	460 (16.26)
Barriers in General	128 (32.16)	134 (33.67)	74 (18.59)	28 (7.03)	34 (8.54)	398 (14.06)
Gender Bias, Gender Gap, Gender Discrimination and Gender Equality	130 (31.25)	136 (32.69)	66 (15.86)	24 (5.78)	60 (14.42)	416 (14.69)
Male Domination	43 (49.43)	14 (16.09)	10 (11.49)	15 (17.24)	5 (5.75)	87 (3.07)
Absence of Women in Decision Making	22 (34.48)	10 (16.13)	12 (19.35)	12 (19.35)	6 (9.69)	62 (2.19)
Skill Shortage	24 (34.28)	18 (25.72)	10 (14.28)	14 (20.01)	4 (5.72)	70 (2.47)

Retention of women in computing	12 (26.67)	14 (31.12)	8 (17.77)	9 (20.00)	2 (4.44)	45 (1.58)
Ways to Attain Equality in Gender Access	24 (41.38)	12 (20.68)	6 (10.35)	2 (3.45)	14 (24.14)	58 (2.05)
Total	**1006 (35.54)**	**994 (35.12)**	**436 (15.40)**	**172 (6.07)**	**223 (7.87)**	**2831 (100)**

Source: Online Resources

Figures in parentheses denote percentage

Data presented in table 40 indicate the source-wise coword usage in Gender Studies in Informatics. It could be noted that out of the total 2831 cowords used in the literature of Gender Studies in Informatics, 35.54 per cent of them are found in conference proceeding form of publication. The reason is conference proceeding constitutes first in order of total paper publications in the field. The coword like women in I. T. Education, women I. T. employment, male domination, absence of women in decision making, skill shortage and ways to attain equity in gender access are mainly reflected in the conference proceeding form of publications in Gender Studies in Informatics.

Out of the total 2831 cowords used in Gender Studies in Informatics, 35.12 per cent of them are covered in journal article form of publications. The majority of the members relating to opportunities to women, initiatives and strategies to promote women's participation under representation of women in employment education and computing, gender bias, gender gap, gender discrimination and gender equity and retention of women in decision making are covered under journal article form of publication. Of the total 2831 key words used in the study, 15.40 per cent of them are published in the form of news item and 6.07 per cent of the cowords are used in project report form of publications. Moreover, 7.87 per cent of the total cowords are published in the form of online discussions.

It could be seen clearly from the above discussion that conference proceeding form of publication occupies the first position in cowords usage in Gender Studies in Informatics, journal article form the second, news item form of publications the third, online discussion form the fourth and project report form the last. The majority of the key words appears in conference proceedings and journal articles since they constitute the major proportion of the total sources of literature in Gender Studies in Informatics.

5
Findings and Conclusion

The findings of the present study lead to the following concluding remarks.

The result of source-wise publication of research output in Gender Studies in Informatics examines the following facts. The conference proceedings form of research output in Gender Studies in Informatics occupies the first in order of reporting, journal article form the second, news item the third, online publications the fourth and project report form of publications the last.

The findings of the continent-wise publication of research output in Gender Studies in Informatics indicate the following facts. The North American continent has contributed the highest number of research output in Gender Studies in Informatics and Australia has taken the lowest position in its contribution of research output. The European continent takes the second order with respect to research output contribution in Gender Studies in Informatics, Asia the third and Africa the fourth.

The findings of continent-wise sources of publication of research output in Gender Studies in Informatics examine the following facts. The African continent's conference proceedings form of publication is less than other continents. The journal articles form of publication is predominant in Asian and European continents and it is conference proceedings cum journal article form publications of Gender Studies in Informatics in Australian and North American Continents.

The findings of country-wise research output performance in Gender Studies in Informatics examine the following facts. South Africa tops the list among the countries in the African continent in publishing research output in Gender Studies in Informatics. Nigeria comes next in position. In the African continent six countries each published only two papers and seven countries each published only one paper during the study period. South Africa alone has sources of published research output.

The findings of country wise research output performance in Gender Studies in Informatics of the Asian continent examine the following facts. It is observed that seven countries have not published conference proceeding form of research output in the Asian continent. Most of the publications are done by Indian scholars. Five countries have not published any paper in journal article form. Among the countries publishing papers in the Asian continent, India and Bangladesh are noteworthy. Eight countries have not published any paper in the form of news item. It is published in three countries, viz., India, Israel and Thailand. Eighth countries have not published any paper in the form of project and it is reported only in three countries. Further five countries have not published any paper in the form of online discussion.

The findings of research output performance of the European continent indicate the following facts. It is seen that England shares more than two-third of the publications in Europe. The Netherlands contributes to considerable level of publications. The remaining sixteen countries share less than 25 per cent of the total output in the European continent. It could be noted that fifteen countries have not published any paper in the form of online discussion and fourteen countries in the form of project and news item form of publications.

The findings of country-wise research output performance of the Australian continent reveal the following facts. It is observed that Australia shares most of the publications in the Australian continent and New Zealand shares only 2 publications of research output in Gender Studies in Informatics.

The findings of country-wise research output performance of the American continent indicate the following facts. USA is a leading contributor of research output in Gender Studies in Informatics. Canada shares a considerable level of research output in Gender Studies in Informatics and the contribution of other countries is quite discouraging as it is less than one per cent each.

The findings of overall relative growth rate of literature in Gender Studies in Informatics examine the following facts. Relative growth rate of publication has shown a declining trend. Consequently the mean doubling time for publications of Gender Studies in Informatics has shown an increasing trend.

The result of the relative growth rate of conference proceeding form of publication indicates the following facts. The mean relative growth rate of conference form of publication has shown a declining trend. Consequently the mean doubling time for publication has also shown a declining trend, due to rapid increase in output during 2000-01 and 2002-03.

The findings of the relative growth rate of conference proceeding form of publications reveal the following facts.

It is observed that the relative growth rate has shown a declining trend. However, it has shown an increasing trend during 1984-85 and 1992-93. Contrastingly, the doubling time for publication has shown an increasing trend in journal article form of publications in research output in Gender Studies in Informatics.

Regarding the result of news item form of publication, the mean relative growth rate of news item form of Gender Studies in Informatics has shown an increasing trend and the mean doubling time for publication has shown a declining trend.

It is observed from the result of analysis that the relative growth rate of project and online discussion form of literature output has shown a declining trend. Contrastingly, the doubling time of publication has shown a massive level of increasing trend.

The findings of continent-wise relative growth rate of publication of research output in Gender Studies in Informatics bring out the following facts.

At the overall level the relative growth rate has shown an increasing trend in the case of research output of North American continent literature whereas the doubling time of publication has shown a declining trend in this connection.

It is observed that the relative growth rate of European continent has shown a declining trend with the exception of the year 1990-91. Contrastingly, the mean doubling time of publications has shown an increasing trend in this connection.

It is seen from the result of the study that the relative growth rate of the Australian continent literature has shown a declining trend whereas the doubling time of publication of literature in Gender Studies in Informatics has shown a declining trend, indicating large time taken in doubling number of research output in Gender Studies in Informatics.

It is observed from the result of the analysis that the relative growth rate of the Asian continent literature has shown a declining trend whereas the doubling time of publication has shown an increasing trend.

The relative growth rate of African continent literature has shown a declining trend. Contrastingly, the doubling time of publications has shown an increasing trend.

The findings of research output performance of South African continent analyze the following facts. The relative position of research output position is quite encouraging in South Africa as it stands above world average and it is considerable in the case of Nigeria. Some countries such as Burkina Faso, Ghana, Mali, Mauritius, Morocco, Sierra Leone and Zambia are at the infancy state with respect to publication of research output in Gender Studies in Informatics.

The findings of journal source-wise research output performance in Gender Studies in Informatics point out the following facts. It is observed that 72 journals have got below the annual average level of publications as per the index value. The noted journals are ACM SIGCSE Bulletin, computer education, computer weekly and gender education as they have more number of publications and also much obtained index score.

The findings of research output performance of conference proved by form of publications indicate the following facts. Among the conference proceedings, ICWES-12, WIT 2002, IFIP 6th, IFIP 4th the noteworthy. In general, all the conference proceedings have got above world annual average level of index value, indicating the predominant position of conference proceedings form of publication in Gender Studies in Informatics.

The result of project form of publications performance in Gender Studies in Informatics indicates the following facts.

Among the total project form of publications, women engineering advisory committee and women networking for education and training in technology have above total of all sources of annual average number of publications. Most of the projects have less number of publications.

Regarding performance of news item form of publications, news item of wired news and business wire are noteworthy in publishing Gender Studies in Informatics. In this study, most of the news item is published each in a paper.

The findings of authorship pattern in Gender Studies in Informatics bring out the following facts. More than two-thirds of the research papers in Gender Studies in Informatics are single authored papers. The double authored papers come next in order, triple authored paper the third, four authored paper the fourth, above five authored papers the fifth and five authored papers the last. It could be noted that when the number of authors increases, their proportion of contributed papers decreases and the vice versa.

It is observed that single authored papers predominate the research output in Gender Studies in Informatics during the study period.

It is also observed from the result of this study that though the degree of collaboration in producing research output in Gender Studies in Informatics is low, it has shown an increasing trend during the study period since it is a new discipline.

The findings of coword analysis in Gender Studies in Informatics show the following facts. It is observed that coword like Barriers, education of computer science among women, women's participation in I.T. Education and training, under representation of women in computing and gender bias. More number of themes relating to barriers, education, gender bias participation, gender gap, women employment initiatives, under representation of women in computing, recognition of women in computing strategies to promote women's participation, gender equity and gender access have appeared mostly during the period 1997-98 and 2002-03. The first period 1982-83 shows varied level of publication of output and cowords occurrence.

The result of continent wise analysis examines the following facts. The North American continent tops the list in using more number cowords in the literature in Gender Studies in Informatics the European continent the second, the Asia continent the third, the Africa continent the fourth and the Australia continent the last.

The findings of source-wise coword use behaviour in literature in Gender Studies in Informatics exhibit the following facts. The conference proceedings top the list of cowords usage since their number of publications is quite large and journal article form of publication comes second with respect to coword used in their publications, new item form of publication takes the third position in their coword use behaviour, online publication form of publications the fourth and the project form of publications the last.

The findings of continent-wise coword usage in Gender Studies in Informatics indicate the following facts. The cowords such as women in I.T. Education, women in I.T. employment, initiatives and strategies to promote women participation in I.T. industry, under representation of women in employment, education and computing and gender bias, gender gap, gender discrimination and gender equity occupy a predominant position in Gender Studies in Informatics as they represent more than 10 per cent each one share in total cowords used in the study. The cowords like opportunities to women, male domination, absence of women in decision making, skill shortage, retention of women in decision making, and ways to attain equity in gender access share less in number with respect to overall cowords used in the study. Among the chosen continents, the North American continent shares 61.92 per cent of the cowords used in Gender Studies in Informatics, Europe comes to next position, Asia the third, followed by Africa.

The findings of coword usage in Gender Studies in Informatics of the African continent examine the following facts. The cowords retention of women's decision making and ways to attain gender equity take more than 10 per cent of global share usage among the African continent scholars. In the African continent cowords appeared only assess 1992-93, because the publication of literature in gender studies informatics shares asses 1992-93. Among the countries in the African continent, Nigeria and South Africa are the major contributors of cowords in Gender Studies in Informatics. The period 1992-93 and 1996-97 have witnessed relatively less number of coword used in Gender Studies in Informatics. Many of the African countries have contributed less than 1 per cent of cowords used in Gender Studies in Informatics during the study period.

It is observed from the results of analysis that the usage of cowords is found to be predominant in the publications of Indian scholars, followed by Philippines. The coword male domination, absence of women in decision making, and opportunities to women, ways to attain equity in gender access have received the attention of scholars of only two Asian countries. The cowords like women in I.T. Education and I.T. employment have received the attention of all scholars of Asian Countries in their published output on Gender Studies in Informatics.

The findings of country-wise coword usage in Gender Studies in Informatics in the European continent reveal the following fats. The cowords have not covered all the eighteen European countries. Among the European countries, the scholars of England occupy the first position in their coverage of all cowords in their publication research output in Gender

Studies in Informatics, followed by the Netherlands. The coword like absence of women in decision making, reference to women in decision making, ways to attain gender equity, and male domination have received the attention of scholars of upto five Asian countries.

The findings of coword usage in Gender Studies in Informatics of the North American continent reflect the following facts. The scholars of the North American continent share more than half of the all cowords usage in literature publishing Gender Studies in Informatics. Among the North American continent countries, the scholars of the USA top the list, followed by Canada in using more proportion of all cowords in their published literature in Gender Studies in Informatics. The cowords like women in I.T. Education and employment have covered the attention of scholars of all chosen countries of the North American continent. Usually, the scholars coword usage level is quite discouraging in contrast in Central America, Eugene, Green Ville, Guatemala, Mexico, Virgina, and West Field, since they have very less number of publications and ultimately they have less coword usage at the global share.

The findings of coword usage in Gender Studies in Informatics of the Australian continent indicate the following facts. Only scholars of the two Australian continent's countries contributed cowords in Gender Studies in Informatics. The New Zealand scholars have not used the coword like skill shortage and male domination. The Australian scholars share a less proportion of all cowords usage at the global level in their published literature in Gender Studies in Informatics, since their number of publications is limited to 24 only.

The findings of duration of coword usage in Gender Studies in Informatics examine the following facts. The highest number of cowords usage is found during the period 1997-98 - 2002-03, due to recording of the highest number of publications in Gender Studies in Informatics. The period 1992-93 to 1996-97 records second in order of cowords share with respect to total number of cowords used in the literature of Gender Studies in Informatics, the period 1987-88 to 1991-92 the third and 1982-83 to 1986-87 the last. The period 1982-83 to 1986-87 is said to be at the infancy stage for the shown literature in Gender Studies in Informatics. Hence this period has a low number of publications and key words usage and thereafter it has grown rapidly particularly during 1997-98 to 2002-03.

The findings of source-wise coword usage in Gender Studies in Informatics indicate the following facts. The conference proceeding form of publication occupy the first position in cowords usage in Gender Studies in Informatics, journal article form the second, news item form of publications the third, online discussion form the fourth and project report form the last. A majority of the key words appeared in conference proceedings and journal articles since they constitute major proportion of the total sources of literature in Gender Studies in Informatics.

It is observed from the study that there would be an enormous scope for emergences of this field as a full-fledged discipline. The rate of growth of publication gives an impression that this field has quite a lot of 'literary warrant' in the years to come.

SUGGESTIONS

The following suggestions are made on the basis of findings of the present study.

1. The research output in gender studies in informatics is quite low in many of the countries in African continent during the study period except South Africa and Nigeria. Hence there is a need to increase the research in Gender Studies in Informatics through Government motivation and financial assistance.

2. Some of the Asian countries have not done research in Gender Studies in Informatics. Hence these countries should motivate the researchers to do research in this area with a view to identify the impact of information technology on women empowerment.
3. Most of the European countries are at the infancy stage of research in Gender Studies in informatics. Hence they should develop research in this field.
4. There is a need to encourage the New Zealand's scholars to do research on Gender Studies in Informatics since their relative contribution is lesser than Australian scholars.
5. The research output in Gender Studies in Informatics is quite low in many of the countries in North American Continent, except USA and Canada. Hence they should develop research in the same field.
6. There is a need to identify the core area of research in Gender Studies in Informatics.
7. There is a need to conduct research studies on impact of information technology on women empowerment at the grass root level.
8. There is a need to establish specific research institutions to promote research in Gender Studies in Informatics in developing countries.
9. In order to promote research in Gender Studies in Informatics, a research centre could be started at the University level.
10. To assess the effectiveness of government's programme of information technology on women empowerment, a specific impact study should be done for this purpose.

RESULT OF HYPOTHESES TESTING

1. The formulated first hypothesis of significant increase in the growth of literature during the period of study is proved as per the result of growth rate analysis.
2. The formulated second hypotheses deals with a significant inter continental and inter country variation in the growth and concentration of research output in Gender Studies in Informatics is proved as per the result of relating growth rate analysis and also co-efficient of variation analysis.
3. The formulated third hypotheses of the cognitive structure of Gender Studies in Informatics varies significantly among the selected continents in the study is proved as per the result of activity index.
4. The formulated fourth hypotheses of significant variation with respect to institutions, producing research output in Gender Studies in Informatics is valid as per the result of tabular data analysis.

Bibliography

Beaver, D.D., "Collaborative and Team Work in Physics," Czechoslouvakia Journal of Physics, Vol., 36, 1986, p. 14.

Bhattacharya, Sujit., "World structure of physics: A cross-national comparison," *JISSI*, 2(1), 1996.

Cabo, Pepin., and **Boersma, Margreet.**, "A keyword analysis of joint biotechnology projects," *JISSI*, 1996

Courtial, J.P., "A co-word analysis of scientometrics," 31(3), 1994, pp.251-260.

Cozzens,S., "U.S.Research assessments : Recent developments, " *Scientometrics*, 34(3), 1995, pp.351-362.

Cronin Blaise., "Women's studies: Bibliometric and content analysis of the formative years," *Journal of documentation*, 53, 1997, pp.123-138.

Dhruv Raina, Gupta B.M, and **Rohit Kandhari.**, "Collaboration in Indian Physics: A case study of the Macro and Micro parametrization of sub-disciplines (1800-1950)," *Scientometrics*, 33(3),1995,pp.295-314.

G.Mahapatra and Bhagvan Das., "Impact of research collaboration on growth of literature in geology: A bibliometric study, *SRELS Journal of information Management*, 37(2), 2000, pp.90-105.

Garg, K.C. and **Padhi, P.**, "A Study of Collaboration in Laser Science and Technology", ***Scientometrics***, 51(2), 2001, pp.415-427.

Grivel, Lue., Mutschke, Peter., Polanco, Xavier "Thematic Mapping on Bibliographical databases by cluster analysis: A description of the SDOC Environment with SOLIS," ***knowl.org,*** 22(2), 1995.

Gupta Davendra, K., "Bibliometric study of literature on Ethiopian librarianship -1944-1992", ***Library Science***,31(4), 1994, pp.208-216.

Gupta, D.K., "Collaboration in Research Output: A Review and a Case Study of Collaborative Trends of Entomological Research in Nigeria," 1900-1973, INICAF, Vol. 1, No. 1, 1986, p. 57.

Humayoon Kabir, S., "Authorship Trend and Solo Research in Bibliometrics: A Bibliometric study", ***Library Science***, 31(2), 1994, pp. 85-90.

Humayoon Kabir., "World literature on bibliometrics: Authorship and Growth pattern," ***ILA Bulletin***,18, 1993, pp.3-4.

Karki MMS., Garg KC., and Sharma praveen., "Activity and growth of organic chemistry in India during 1971-1989," ***Scientometrics***, 49(2),2000,pp.278-278.

Ketty Rodriguez, and **Moreiro JA.**, "Growth and Development of Research in the Field of Ecology; as Measured by Dissertation Title Analysis"; ***Scientometrics***, 35(1), 1996, pp. 56-70.

Kostoff Ronald N., Fberhart, Henry J., and **Toothman Darrell Ray**., "Data Base Tomography for technical intelligence : A Road map of the near- earth space science and technology Literature," ***Information processing and managemen***t, 34(1),1988,pp. 69-85.

Macias-Chapula,Cesar A and **Muangos-Nolasco Acacia**.., "Bibliometric analysis of AIDS literature in Central

Africa", *Scientometrics,* 54(2), 2002, pp.309-317.

Maheswarappa B. S, and **Ningoli M.H.**, "Growth of literature in the field of applied sciences in India (1965-89)," *INICAF,* 12, 1993, pp.192-200.

Maheswarappa, B.S., et al., "Collaborative Research in Science and Technology: A Bibliometric Study," *Journal of Library and Information Science,* Vol. 9, No. 2, 1984, pp. 154-159.

Michelet Bertrand and **Turner W.A..**, "Co-word search: A system for information retrieval," *Journal of information science,* 1985, pp.173-181.

Noyons, E.C.M., and **Can Raan, A.F.J.**, "Bibliometric cartography of scientific and technological developments of an R&D field," *Scientometrics,* 30(1), (1994) pp.157-173

Parvathamma, N and **Gunjal, S.R.**, "Growth pattern of Literature and Scientific productivity of authors in Indian Earth Science 1978-88: A Bibliometric study", *Library Science,* 30(2), 1993, pp.54-63.

Planco, Xavier and **Grivel,Luc.**, "Mapping knowledge: The use of co-word analysis techniques for mapping a sociology data file of four publishing countries,"*JISSI,*1(2),1995.

Preveen Sharma, and **K.C Garg.**, "Bibliometrics of Solar Power Research in India", *IASLIC Bulletin,* 38(4), 1993, pp.155-169.

Ramakrishna N.V., "Bibliometrics of Animal Cell Culture Technology Literature; A Study Based on the Animal Cell Biotechnology," *Annals of Library Science and Documentation,* 46(3), 1991, pp.81-96.

Rana Madan, S and **Agarwal, Sunita.**, "Authorship trends in India wildlife and fisheries literature – A bibliometric study", *Annals of Library Science and Documentation,* 41(1), 1994, pp.13-18.

Rikken ,F., kiers, H.A.L., and **Vos, R.,** "Mapping the dynamics of adverse drug reactions in subsequent time periods," ***Scientometrics,*** 33 (3), 1995, pp.367-380.

Sridhar, M.S., "A Study of Co-authorship and Collaborative Research among Indian Space Technologists, R.D. Management," Vol. 15, No. 3, 1985, pp. 231-237.

Tijssen R.J.W., and ***Van Raan A.F.J.,*** "Mapping co-word structures: A comparison of multidimensional scaling and leximappe," ***Scientometrics,*** 15(3-4), 1989, pp.283-295.

Tijssen, Robert J.W., "A quantitative assessment of interdisciplinary structures in science and technology: co-classification analysis of energy research", ***Research policy,*** 1992, pp. 27- 44.

Tijssen, Robert J.W., and **Vanraan, Anthony F.J,.** "Mapping changes in S &T: Bibliomtric Co-occurrence analysis of the R&D Literature," ***Evaluation Review,*** 18(1), 1994, pp. 98-115.

Ying Ding, Gobinda G. Chowdhury, Schubert Foo., "Bibliography of information retrieval research by using co-word analysis," ***Information Processing & Management,*** 37, 2000, pp 817-842.